THE MASTER ARCHITECT SERIES

# HARTMAN-COX

Selected and Current Works

THE MASTER ARCHITECT SERIES

# HARTMAN·COX

## Selected and Current Works

First published in Australia in 1994 by
The Images Publishing Group Pty Ltd
ACN 059 734 431
6 Bastow Place, Mulgrave, Victoria, 3170
Telephone (61 3) 561 5544 Facsimile (61 3) 561 4860

National Library of Australia Cataloguing-in-Publication Data

Hartman, George E.
    Hartman-Cox: selected and current works.

    Bibliography.
    Includes index.
    ISBN 1 875498 14 1
    Master Architect Series ISSN 1320 7253

    1. Hartman, George E. 2. Cox, Warren J.
    3. Hartman-Cox (Firm). 4. Architecture, Modern—20th
    century—United States. 5. Architects—United States.
    6. Architecture, American. I. Cox, Warren J.
    II. Title. (Series: Master architect series).

720.92

Edited by Stephen Dobney
Designed by The Graphic Image Studio Pty Ltd,
Mulgrave, Australia
Printed by Southbank Pacific Pty Ltd,
Fishermans Bend, Australia

# Contents

# Introduction

*Richard Guy Wilson, University of Virginia*
*This is an edited version of a longer essay by R.G.Wilson entitled*
*'Towards an Architecture of Civility, Competency and Context*
*with Creativity – An Analysis of Hartman-Cox'.*

The work of George Hartman and Warren Cox and their firm Hartman-Cox provides an instructive commentary on the nature of American architecture in the late twentieth century. In many ways their work stands as a challenge to many of the modernist beliefs that have dominated much of the twentieth century. Listening to a different muse, Hartman-Cox appear to have gone backwards, and have relegitimized the use of historical imagery and style, those elements supposedly buried in the dustbins of history.

Hartman-Cox's work arouses passions—positive and negative. It appears regularly in architectural journals and newspaper critiques and is highly valued by their clients, many of whom return to the firm with subsequent commissions. In over 25 years of practice they have won over 90 design awards, and in 1988 they received the American Institute of Architects Architectural Firm Award. For many admirers their architecture represents good manners and civility; they practice a design approach which respects and enhances the context. Understandably, their work is a joy to many preservationists and urbanists.

Some critics, however, lambaste Hartman-Cox for their historicism and disavowal of modernist ideology. Some feel that Hartman-Cox's absence of a common look indicates they have no convictions about their stance— that they simply react to context. Some of their work, especially that which recalls classicism, has been labelled "radical conservative", while their super-scale five-story Roman Doric peristyle at Market Square verges on "fascistic" according to one critic.

Then there is their location: Hartman-Cox play in the minor leagues charge some critics; they are regionalists located in Washington, DC, an isolated backwater. They are the leading members of a group sometimes called the "Washington School" although their practice is now a national one.

Of these criticisms, the partners accept a few and shrug off the others as misguided. Warren Cox pointedly asserts that "the work of Hartman-Cox is deliberately marked by the lack of a recognizable office style and by a variety of response." Noting the variety of their commissions—from office buildings to churches, houses and educational buildings—and the historical context of Washington, DC, Cox claims that they attempt to honor the special sites of their buildings and the clients' programs, rather than ignore or oppose them. "We want to do buildings that are nice, that enhance environments rather than destroy them." Their approach is to see the city as the object of concern instead of treating the building as an isolated object.

Although Hartman-Cox were early defectors from orthodox modernism and are frequently lumped with the post-modernists, they have resisted identification with that movement or with any specific architectural group or theoretical position.

George Hartman and Warren Cox view architecture as a service profession: the architect's duty is both to serve the client and to design for the larger community. Architecture is an art, but it serves higher goals than the creator's ego: it is a representation of community values. Contextualism to them means making buildings sensitive to their location. Both partners have been active on the lecture and jury circuit and have held visiting critic positions at various universities, but primarily they are designers.

The firm was established in 1965 and comprises the two senior partners, a junior partner, Mario Boiardi, and two associates, Lee Becker and Graham Davidson. Their offices in the Georgetown district are surprisingly modest in contrast to some architects' offices: no cut-out columns, classical details or fancy pilastered library, but rather simple and basic to the point of austerity.

They have no marketing or business manager; business is taken care of early in the morning or over lunch once a week. The partners claim this is ideal; it eliminates an entire level of unnecessary and expensive management. The size of the firm has varied, from a staff of 30 during the building boom of the 1980s to its current size of 18 architects, an office manager, Marian Holmes, and a secretary. They handle about five major projects a year and, to a large degree, can be selective about the projects they take on. In the early years of the firm they did dozens of remodelings, additions and suburban houses. Although both partners insist they would still do a private house, they have specialized in commissions for image-conscious developers and cultural and educational institutions. They are hired on the basis of their reputation as architects who can design in sensitive surroundings.

For Hartman-Cox the interview process is important. Both partners plan each interview and they prepare extensively, deciding on the design strategy and the scheme. In the interview the partners try to persuade the client they are doing what he wants, so the client will not be surprised as the design develops. They pride themselves on competent design and producing buildings with which the client is happy.

Programming is an important element of the design process for Hartman-Cox. In a sense the logical outcome of modern functionalism, programming involves the rigorous analysis of a client's demands and needs and the inter-relationships of the different functions. Hartman and Cox feel that programming puts a burden on the client to impose some order on their requirements, and for the architect it reduces the variables. As Warren Cox observes, "Programming tells you more than you ever wanted to know about a project", but he also points out that part of the success of designs such as the National Humanities Center or the H.E. Butt Headquarters comes from a rigorous programming study.

In the Hartman-Cox office the same team stays with a project from the beginning to the end. Design development is not separated from production and can therefore be left open much longer. "Buildings sometimes design themselves," explains Warren Cox. George Hartman feels that experience gives the designer confidence to allow things to happen rather than forcing a solution. Confidence and the concept of trying to serve the client mean that the client is listened to. With candor, George Hartman recalls that they originally designed the Euram Building in concrete and gray glass, but the owner insisted on changing it to brick and regular glass. "He was correct," Hartman claims, "Concrete would have been awful on the corner of Dupont Circle."

An understanding of history and precedent plays a large role in the design process. Both Hartman and Cox continue to study history and they have traveled extensively. History does not just mean styles, but also a knowledge of building types and their variations, which provides another contextual clue. When given a project such as the Winterthur Museum extension, a range of prototypical solutions were examined. In this case, the expansion of an already vastly expanded and rambling building, and the necessity of bridging a stream, made a design loosely based on a Loire Valley chateau (Chenonceaux) one answer. While Chenonceaux is a source, the Hartman-Cox design contains features reminiscent of Italianate buildings and also of Richard Morris Hunt's Goelet house in Newport.

Computers have been introduced into the office, but the major method of design comes through drawings and models. Presentation perspectives are made either in-house or by an outside professional. Much more central to design development at Hartman-Cox are models. Elaborate site models are created that include the surroundings. A design critique may involve studying the breaks in a mansard roof and how that curve meets the surroundings and the sky.

The linking of design and production has led to an intense interest in the craft of building: an understanding about materials, their possibilities and limitations. This permits Hartman-Cox to get high quality results, as with the Georgetown University Edward Bennett Williams Law Library, where the material might be mistaken for cut limestone rather than lowly concrete. Flexible urethane molds allow for the design of elaborate pre-cast concrete panels, as used in Pennsylvania Plaza. Hartman-Cox's interest in the craft of building is obvious when Pennsylvania Plaza is compared with many of its modern neighbors which lack any finesse in detail.

Details and how they are to be made—or supplied—are studied intensively by the designers. Hartman-Cox's work shows a progressive sophistication in detail and ornamentation. Up to the mid-1970s their work is typical of the time; details were both simple and minimal. The big shift for the firm began in 1976 when they started renovating the Folger Shakespeare Library. Designed by Paul Cret in 1928–29, the Folger was a high point of the classical moderne (Greco-Deco) mode in Washington, DC. During the process of restoration and rehabilitation, Hartman-Cox replicated the original details of Cret's building, and then adapted them for their new addition. Hartman-Cox's new details are of several types: explicit copy-book replications of Doric order for oak columns; reinterpreted or "free classical" Doric scaled down for reading room table legs; and transposition, taking what were originally limestone quoins and picking them out in rough plaster.

For George Hartman and Warren Cox, exposure to the idea of modernism began in college, where they began to form their architectural ideals. They both studied art history as undergraduates, and both heard the party line that when it came to the twentieth century, there was only one answer: modernism. But history brought up problems: Cox wrote his undergraduate honors thesis on Le Corbusier's early work at La Chaux-de-Fonds, Switzerland. This was the unknown Le Corbusier, the past he forgot when he discovered the machine and became a modernist. Cox later published photos of this forgotten and traditionalist Le Corbusier in *Perspecta* (1960), which he helped edit.

Princeton in Hartman's time was still under the sway of a late beaux-arts tradition personified by Jean Labatut. "Laby", as he was known, did not teach a style, Hartman recalls; instead his direction was always the relationship with the surroundings, "the thousands of relationships with things . . . made the building richer." The most important influence on Hartman was Enrico Peressutti of the Italian firm BBPR. With his partner, Ernesto Rogers, Peressutti founded the neo-liberty movement which tried to establish a modernism that drew upon tradition and local atmosphere. Peressutti reinforced Labatut's concern with site and surroundings, and at the same time had a diverting sense of humor; a belief that architecture could be fun. He also stressed that buildings were real, not just an exercise on paper or an idea, but brick and mortar.

Rogers (Peressutti's partner) also brought the neo-liberty message to Cox at Yale. Rogers received a standing ovation from the students when he praised Yale's colleges of the 1920s which were in a variety of Tudor, Jacobean, Georgian and other styles and which were regularly lambasted by the studio critics. As a result of his father's earlier acquaintance with Rogers, Cox spent two summers in Italy working for BBPR.

Out of school and into practice by the mid-1960s in Washington, DC, Hartman and Cox followed many of the currents then prominent in American architecture. They did their share of additions to houses in the "backyard sweepstakes" of those years. Their preferred image was elegantly simple and abstract, detail was minimal, exteriors were white painted brick or flush board. The neo-Corbusian white box revived by Richard Meier and others and known as the New York School was investigated by Hartman-Cox in the Conant residence in Potomac. Although owing an obvious debt to Le Corbusier, Hartman and Cox also illustrated an independence of mind: the long side elevation is reminiscent of Richard Neutra's Lovell Health House, while the end elevation with the large circular window is pure minimalist art.

A different image began to appear in a number of other structures Hartman-Cox designed and built in the late 60s and early 70s. Stylistically these were hybrids, a low-key modernism that appeared across the country and ironically was claimed to be regional. The overall formalist strategy was the utilization of the diagonal in plan, elevation and section. The diagonal, or "zoot" as it was popularly known, captured the imagination of American architects during this period causing countless shed roofs, splayed and angular entrance ways, and contorted plans. The fascination with the diagonal had an origin in the late work of Alvar Aalto, who was very popular in America in these years; equally it was a reaction to the rigid ninety degree angle of the International Style. Also influential was Sea Ranch and the other early work of Moore, Lyndon, Turnbull and Whitaker in California. Both Hartman and Cox remember being amazed at Charles Moore's early work, a reinvigoration of a native San Francisco Bay Area regionalism.

These sources, along with the Italian neo-liberty, came together in a positive way at the Mount Vernon Chapel, which responds sensitively to its site—a steep ravine. Certain features of the front elevation, especially the continuous short vertical and long horizontal, are reminiscent of Frank Lloyd Wright. Hartman and Cox spent time looking at American colonial churches as a source for the interior which, in spite of its dramatically diagonal roof and opening to the exterior, exudes a peaceful calm, evoking the space of early Congregationalist churches. This regionalist modernism is also apparent at the nearby dormitories Hartman-Cox designed for Mount Vernon College.

The Euram Building at Dupont Circle, in Washington, DC, and the National Humanities Center at Research Triangle Park in North Carolina have traits similar to this low-key, regional modernism. The Euram Building reflects its oddly shaped site (common in Washington) and the adjacent brick structures. The contrast of brick and exposed concrete beams and post-tensioned girders is indebted to Louis Kahn, but the Euram escapes the trap of mimicry that bedeviled so many architects in those years. The National Humanities Center of a few years later has a dominant plan that works marvellously well, indeed it looks like a plan diagram exploded into three dimensions.

By the mid-1970s the term post-modernism had arrived on the American architectural scene and, while nobody could agree on its tenets, it served as a rallying cry among the younger generation—those in their 30s and 40s—to openly flout the traditional modernist pieties.

Hartman-Cox were already a step ahead of the post-modernist/ contextualist wave, as can be seen in the National Permanent Building (Washington, DC, 1977). Located on a prominent Pennsylvania Avenue site which could be seen from a great distance, it called for an appropriate scale and massing. Cox describes it as very neo-liberty in origin, and to some degree it owes a debt in inspiration to BBPR and also to Franco Albini's work from 15 years earlier. But the immediate inspiration for National Permanent lay with a building one block away down Pennsylvania Avenue, the Old Executive Office Building (formerly State, War and Navy) by Alfred B. Mullett, 1871–88. The inclined roof with diagonal ducts, the concrete columns and perforated trusses with recessed windows are all abstractions of Mullett's creation.

## Washington, DC

Although changing architectural sensibilities played a role in the
development of Hartman-Cox, another key to their development
lies in the location of most of their work: Washington, DC.
Washington is more than a place; it is a state of mind. As George
Hartman says, "It enforces an attitude." Well known, of course,
is the plan of Washington by Major Pierre Charles L'Enfant,
a French baroque scheme later modified by Burnham, McKim
and Olmsted. L'Enfant's plan of a grid crossed by radials created
a variety of oddly shaped building sites—triangles, convex and
concave lots that call for special adaptation, such as the Octagon
by William Thornton or the Euram. Washington's wide avenues
provide an opportunity for the creation of spatial signifiers,
for towers, turrets and porticos that measure or terminate vistas.

Washington, DC, became an eye-opener for, as Warren Cox
remembers, "We ended up just liking the old buildings better."
Cox had the chance to investigate Washington's older
architecture in the mid-1960s when he co-edited the
*AIA Guide to Washington, DC.* There was "a great stash of really
terrific neo-classical, beaux-arts Washington buildings dating
from about 1895 to the Federal Triangle," which, as Cox recalls,
nobody paid any attention to. Reinforcing this attitude was the
service of both partners on different review boards, the approval
of which was needed to put up any building in the District.
Working both sides of the street, as architects and reviewers,
they began to question, as George Hartman put it, "whether the
building you are putting up is as good as the one you are taking
down." They recognized that the scaleless and blank facades of
buildings such as their Euram did not stack up well against the
older structures, and that the only thing that saved them was
Washington's height limit. On the Euram Building, Cox observes:
"If it had been bigger, it would have been a nightmare."
They found themselves as natural allies in the growing
preservation movement of the 1960s.

Washington enforced an attitude on the architects who paid attention; as Hartman observes: "We have an obligation to ensure that Washington doesn't become Disneyland, and also that it is different from London, Paris, Rome." The lesson of Washington is a lesson of civility, or understanding the context and the *genius loci*. The consequence for Hartman-Cox is that the totality of the city is more important than the individual building as an object. Too many modern architects completely denied anything that had come before; they were always beginning again. Hartman claims that "the L'Enfant plan is more valuable than any single building, and that some buildings and some squares are more important than others."

What Hartman and Cox have discovered from their urban work in Washington is the constant need for variety: that the American city is made up of many small pieces; that elements of the older city—the Victorian city—such as the towers of prominent corner buildings, were worth reviving, that they marked location and measured distances.

In some circumstances "there shouldn't be a statement," says Cox. Instead of statements the key, as in their Sumner School complex, is keeping the scale of the street and reintroducing the intricate detail that any older streetscape contains. Cox notes that "especially in tight urban spaces . . . you can hardly make things too small." In working with significant older buildings the new work must be reticent; the architect must hide the intervention.

Beginning in the mid-1970s a few developers realized that a sexy architectural image helped to lease space at a top price—a high profile design could earn money. George Hartman claims that a great deal of the credit must go to Philip Johnson. Johnson's highly publicized work with the developer Gerald Hines showed others that instead of putting up the cheapest building imaginable, image and perceived quality could be important. In Washington developers became aware that how buildings looked was important: that the facade, lobby and wash rooms mattered to clients. Most office building design is unconcerned with the interior, which is divided up and designed after the lease is signed. Attention is concentrated on the exterior and the lobby. Warren Cox has heretically claimed that, in the case of office building, architects are often "exterior decorators, or wallpaper architects"; they simply wrap the box.

1001 Pennsylvania Avenue is a buff brick cloak that has a parentage of turn-of-the-century commercial office buildings with a base, middle and top (or cornice). The middle section, or the shaft, is articulated by a vertical 1-2-1 bay rhythm—projecting columns frame inset double bays. On its side street elevations the building also incorporates a number of facades from pre-existing turn-of-the-century buildings.

Further down Pennsylvania Avenue is Market Square with its giant Roman Doric colonnade, actually a curtain for offices, apartments and commercial space. The difference in outer dress is explained by three circumstances: it is a background for the Navy Memorial; it is across from John Russell Pope's National Archives (1935); and it frames one of Washington's most important vistas that terminates in the Old Patent Office Building with its magnificent Greek revival facade by Robert Mills and others (1836; now the National Portrait Gallery).

Another Washington box by Hartman-Cox is 4250 Connecticut Avenue which responds to a different set of circumstances. Stylistically in the streamlined mode, the stacked forms recall an abstract ocean liner, an image common to the 1930s nautical moderne. The standard concrete steel frame is wrapped with a buff brick, responding to the nearby University of the District of Columbia campus, while the art deco banding refers to a 1930s shopping center across the street. The long streamlined form picks up the flow of traffic along Connecticut at this point. Its massing has more articulation than many Washington boxes since it serves as a metro entrance.

**Stylistic Matters**

Notions of style and *zeitgeist* play an important role in Hartman-Cox's work as it has developed. They began to recognize in the 1970s that a controlling modern idiom did not exist, that the center had not held. The new reigning center for American architecture would be to preserve the best while designing and adding creatively. This seems to be the *zeitgeist* for Hartman-Cox: a self-effacing preservation design when the foreground is strong, such as at the Sumner School complex, or more dramatic when there is a need for a statement, as at Market Square.

The consequence for Hartman-Cox of working in Washington, DC, has been an attitude that is applicable elsewhere. This has meant in some cases almost literal replication, as at Brown University where they duplicated the exterior form and details in an addition to the John Carter Brown Library. Different in overall approach, but with a similar respect for the original, was their conversion (in association with another firm) of a former US Army arsenal into a campus-like headquarters for the H.E. Butt Grocery Company in San Antonio.

Style becomes a tool for making relationships, for fostering attitudes and making statements. Understanding the original motivations becomes important when designing additions.

The Chrysler Museum in Norfolk is a case in point. The building was originally designed as an Italian palazzo in the 1930s by local Norfolk architects, but never finished. In the 1960s a wing and tower were added. The additions of the 1970s in a concrete brutalist manner had turned the museum into an inhospitable and alienating experience. Given that most American art museums are clothed in some form of classicism, Hartman-Cox's choice to return to the original intentions became obvious.

The multiplicity of styles and forms of facades gave the American city its character. At Pennsylvania Plaza Hartman-Cox were faced with a large site on which the typical developer's block would crush the intricate surroundings. This is exactly what had happened next door where the architects, Eisenman-Robertson, had neglected to study the context. Hartman-Cox had already done work on the site restoring and adapting the old Apex (Central National Triangle) Building and its neighbors, each in their own individual style. The program Hartman-Cox was given called for residential and office space, hence they split the structure visually and functionally into two distinct parts. The office side is articulated as a nineteenth century Italianate loft, originally constructed out of cast iron, now made in pre-cast panels. The apartment half is faced in red and buff brick, the wall is articulated with window bays or oriels, and the end elevation terminated with a tower. Instead of large-scale monotony, the building provides a variety of facades and incidents.

Although Hartman-Cox eschew an identification with post-modernism, they are clearly heirs of the loosening of modernism's stranglehold. They have largely remained oblivious to what could be called "comic strip post-modernism", though features have popped up in some buildings, such as the paper-thin new entrance fragment in the Sumner Square. Their design for the Gallery Row staircase in Washington displays the change of floor level in a whimsical manner, and at times they have ironically and intentionally misused features, such as at Market Square where the metopes common in Roman Doric entablatures have become windows.

Hartman and Cox take pride in making good buildings, in designs that work and solve the clients' problems, but also make a contribution to the environment. They are professionals who, as Cox says, "do buildings that are nice. If you have a nice old building that you don't want screwed up, we are a good choice for an addition."

The partners like to claim that they lack a particular ideology—
"Ideology leads you around by the nose," Cox emphasizes.
However, they do have an ideology of sorts—an approach born
of designing in complicated situations. Their ideology involves the
immediate surroundings and the larger city. There is an elitism in
their position, in their decisions about hierarchy and what should
be emphasized, for example that a library should look like an
institution of culture and not a branch department store. This is
where Hartman-Cox fit: they have emerged as one of the strong
voices speaking for traditional imagery and for a positive role of
the individual building within its context.

Although Hartman-Cox reject the notion of a "signature style"—
that all the work coming out of an office should have a common
look—they do have certain trademarks, such as a reliance upon
a loose classicism and a finesse with details. A building by
Hartman-Cox looks very different from one by Robert A.M. Stern,
Allan Greenberg, or Venturi-Scott-Brown. George Hartman and
Warren Cox make some of the most interesting architecture
being produced in America today. They have helped to change
the architectural face of America in making historicism
respectable again.

Modernism has been the great debate of the last 50 years in
American architecture. In spite of modernism's seeming
expulsion from the garden of Eden for a period it has returned
and continues to attract followers. Great and compelling designs
still continue to be built under the different flags of modernism.
But undeniable is the fact that in many ways it was brutal, even
destructive to the American city. The appropriate place for
modern design is in its own landscape; it has both positive and
negative qualities.

It is time to revise our view of modern. Only in the hands of
the polemicists did it become a closed system. Instead of having
one style it encompassed many styles over the past two centuries.
Change and experiment are part of its core, and the re-revival
of historical styles was inevitable. Modern is not just the surface
treatment but includes structure, heating, ventilation, air
conditioning, flexibility and light.

Sensory changes have occurred and the world will never be the
same again. Perhaps Hartman-Cox are more modern than those
architects still clinging to outmoded styles.

# Selected and Current Works

# Private Residence, Phillips/Brewer House

Design/Completion 1967/1969
7705 Connecticut Avenue
Chevy Chase, Maryland
Phillips/Brewer families
3,500 square feet
Wood frame
Painted plywood with battens; cedar shingle roof;
wood, carpet and tile floors; exterior brick paving

This house sits on a small corner lot, long thought unbuildable, which is entered off an attractive cul-de-sac at its inside corner. There are major highways on two sides of the site. The other two sides face a neo-colonial subdivision of high density.

The program called for privacy, both internal and external, and three distinct areas, each to be reached without going through another: a suite for the mother and grandmother; a bedroom and bath for the college-age son; and living, dining and kitchen areas. Fenced yards were to be provided for pets and outdoor privacy.

As designed, the house is basically two wings pitched at right angles to each other. The entry is at the corner where the wings connect, and contains a circular stair leading to the son's second floor area. The mother and grandmother's suite opens to the left, and the public areas are entered to the right. The house has three courtyards. The largest, off the public areas, retains an existing elm tree and is shielded by a pergola which follows the roof shapes. The other two are smaller and are off the library and dining room.

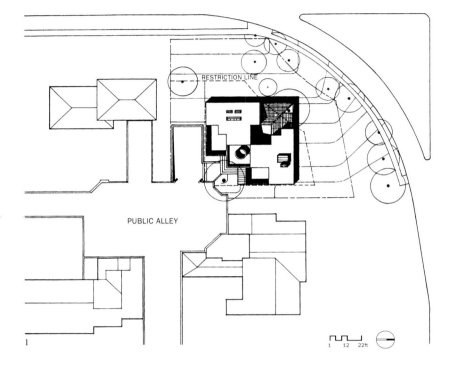

1

2

20

1 Site plan
2 From the neighboring house
3 First floor plan
4 Second floor plan
5 Entrance off Cul de sac

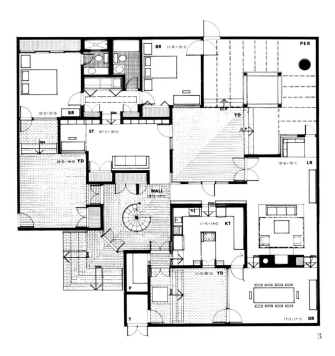

3

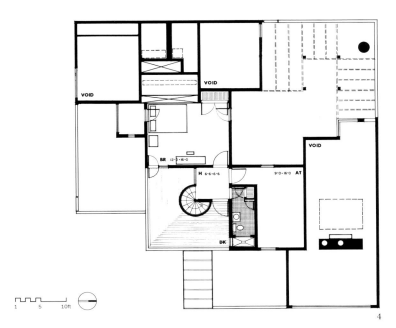

4

5

6

8

9

10

8  Courtyard
9  Entrance
10  House from intersection
11  Detail of end wall

Private Residence, Phillips/Brewer House   25

# College Chapel, Mount Vernon College

Design/Completion 1967/1970
2100 Foxhall Road, NW
Washington, DC
Mount Vernon College
7,500 square feet
Masonry bearing wall and steel frame
Brick; steel casements; slate and painted
standing seam metal roofs; brick paving;
wood and carpet floors

The entry to the chapel is at the top
of a 30-foot ravine, while the bulk of the
chapel slips down into the ravine itself.
The upper, entrance elevation is relatively
closed and, while abstract, uses brick and
punched windows similar to those on the
existing neo-colonial buildings on the
campus. The building's west side, by
contrast, consists of a vast sloping grid
of clerestories that bathe the sanctuary
in diffuse natural light. The building,
while three and a half stories high inside,
is seen as only a story and a half from
the campus and as one story from the
neighboring residential street.

The architects wanted to create an
unsentimental "luminous but placid
interior" appropriate to the program,
which stipulated its use for both religious
and secular purposes. Because the
sanctuary was intended for a variety
of purposes, its plan was designed to be
flexible: chairs and an altar/performance
area can be moved as befits the event.
Seating for 300 is in three sections
around the altar, the wall beyond which
is transparent and overlooks the woods
and a stream.

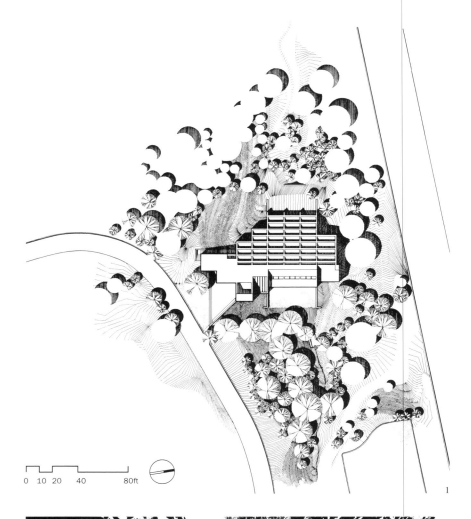

0  10 20  40       80ft

1

2

1 Site plan
2 East elevation
3 Transverse section
4 View from playing field/entrance level

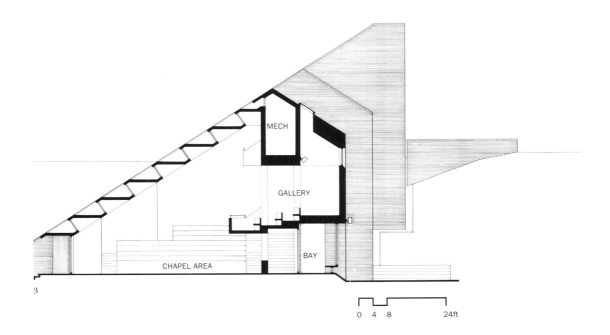

MECH

GALLERY

BAY

CHAPEL AREA

3

0  4  8            24ft

4

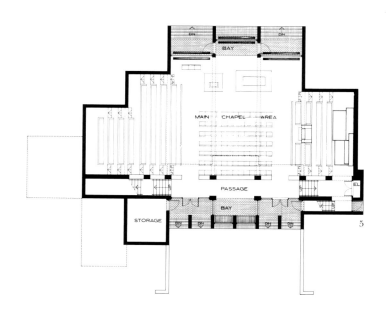

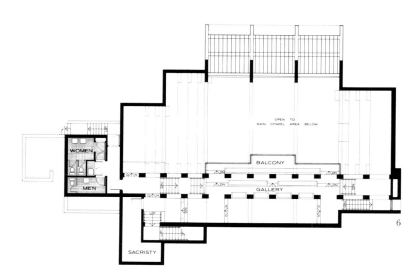

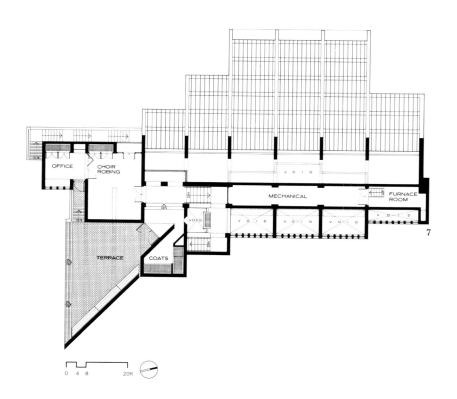

0  4  8        20ft

5   Plan lower level
6   Plan middle level
7   Plan upper level
8   From the glade towards the altar: west elevation
9   Chapel nave

8

9

# Tennis Building, St Alban's School

Design/Completion 1968/1970
National Cathedral Grounds
Washington, DC
St Alban's School
1,600 square feet
Brick bearing wall and wood frame
Brick; custom wood trim; membrane roof

The constraints on this tiny structure were abundant. The site on the National Protestant Episcopal Cathedral grounds occupies a corner between the St Alban's tennis courts, which are backed by an eight-foot-high retaining wall, and an existing concrete stair, leading to the school's baseball/football field.

The architects began by stretching a long walkway with seating atop the retaining wall behind the courts. The building was designed as a gatehouse, and the walkway passes down through it. Inside, the walkway is topped by a skylight. To the rear of the upper level is a tennis shop and club office with storage, while an open viewing stand faces the courts. Below these are toilets and locker rooms for both courts and playing fields.

1

1   Passage to playing fields and walkways
2   South elevation
3   From the courts
4   Main floor plan

2

3

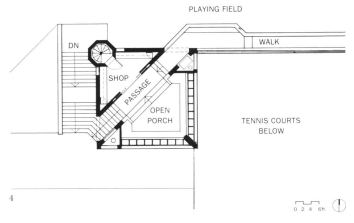

4

PLAYING FIELD

DN

SHOP

WALK

PASSAGE

OPEN
PORCH

TENNIS COURTS
BELOW

0 2 4   6ft

# Euram Building

Design/Completion 1968/1971
21 Dupont Circle, NW
Washington, DC
The Euram Corporation
Washington, DC
75,000 square feet (including parking)
Reinforced concrete frame; post-tensioned
perimeter beams
Exposed architectural concrete; brick; fixed,
top and bottom supported, half-inch plate glass
windows; quarry tile paving

An initial, if abstract, step toward a
contextually determined commercial
architecture, the eight-story Euram
Building was designed to echo the
massing, scale, colors and materials
of the neighboring buildings around
Dupont Circle. The red brick and
concrete elevations reflect the Dupont
Circle Building next door, while the
re-entrant facade and bridge over the
entrance come from Stanford White's
Washington Club across the Circle.

The building was configured around
a triangular, light-filled atrium. A simple
program of generic office spaces
prompted a design that expresses the
building's principal elements—its vertical
circulation; its lobby, office and service
spaces; and, particularly, its structure.
The bridge-like exposed concrete beams
and post-tensioned girders spanning
brick corner piers are a direct expression
of the Euram Building's columnless
undergirding. Originally designed with
gray glass, clear glass was substituted at the
owner's insistence. This change clarified
the design, allowing a clearer reading
of solid and void, particularly at night.

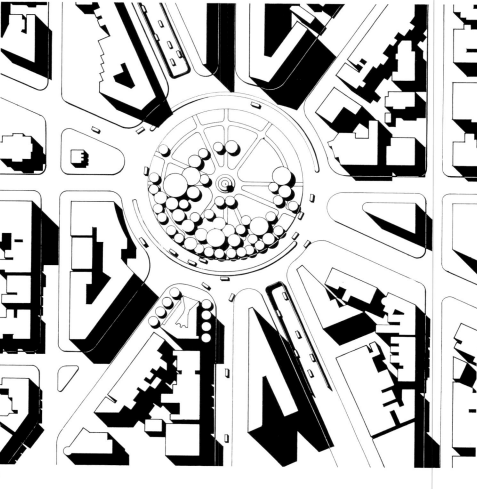

1

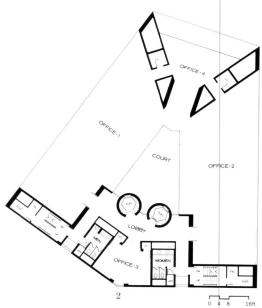

2

1   Site plan
2   Seventh floor plan
3   North elevation at night

0   4   8        16ft

3

4

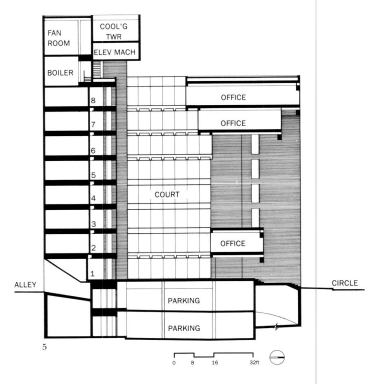

FAN ROOM | COOL'G TWR
BOILER | ELEV MACH
8 | OFFICE
7 | OFFICE
6 |
5 |
4 | COURT
3 |
2 | OFFICE
1 |
ALLEY | PARKING | CIRCLE
| PARKING |

5

0　8　16　32ft

6

7

8

# College Dormitory, Mount Vernon College

Design/Completion 1969/1972
2100 Foxhall Road, NW
Washington, DC
Mount Vernon College
25,000 square feet
Masonry bearing wall and precast concrete plank
Brick; steel casements; slate roof

The existing campus, comprising 1940s neo-Georgian red brick buildings with gray slate roofs, is situated on a rolling site in a suburban-style residential neighborhood. Asked to relate their dormitory in scale and materials to existing structures on the campus, the architects designed an abstract brick building whose campus side is brick, while its south and east elevations cascade down a hillside in twin attached "V" shapes, clad in slate and indented with balconies.

The building's two units contain housing for 48 students, and common rooms, seminar rooms, laundries, etc. Dormitory rooms, each with a terrace and a skylight placed over a desk, face away from the campus for the sake of privacy and have views of a wooded valley. Seminar and common rooms overlook the entrance quadrangle.

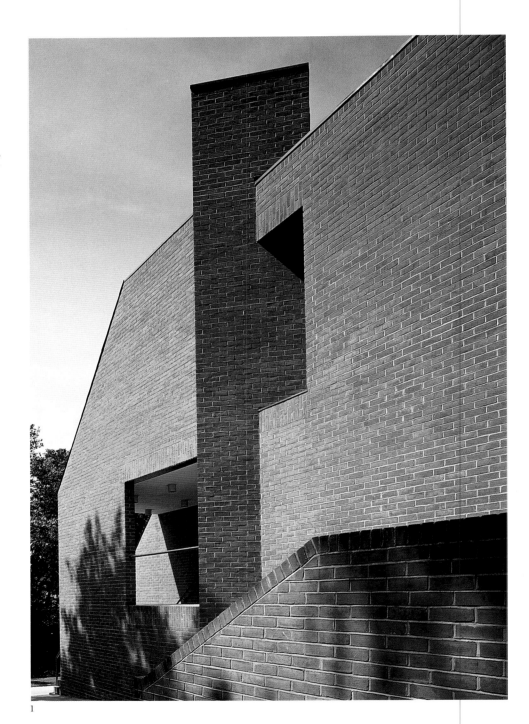

1

1   Detail of end wall
2   North or entrance elevation
3   Site plan

2

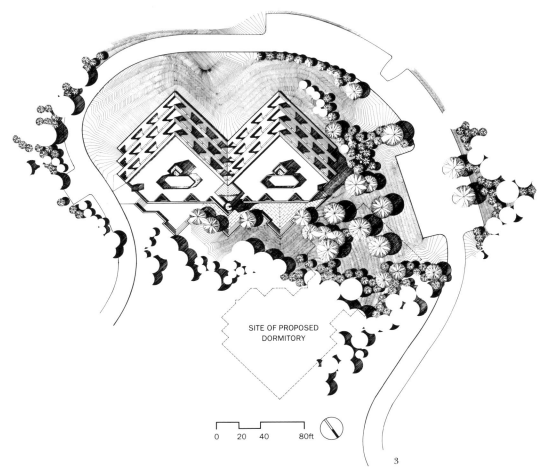

SITE OF PROPOSED
DORMITORY

0  20  40    80ft

3

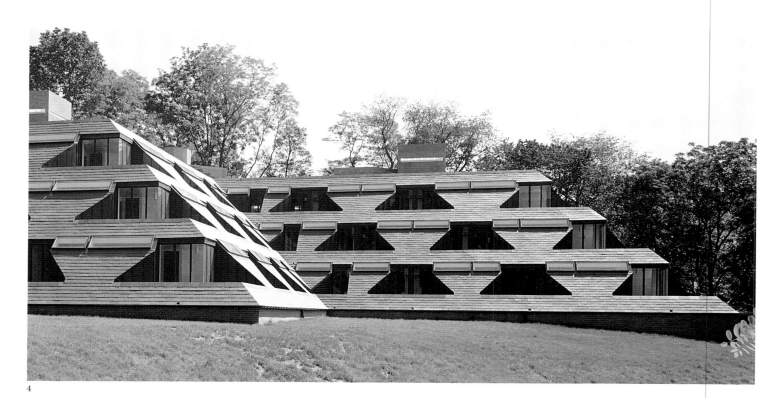

4

5

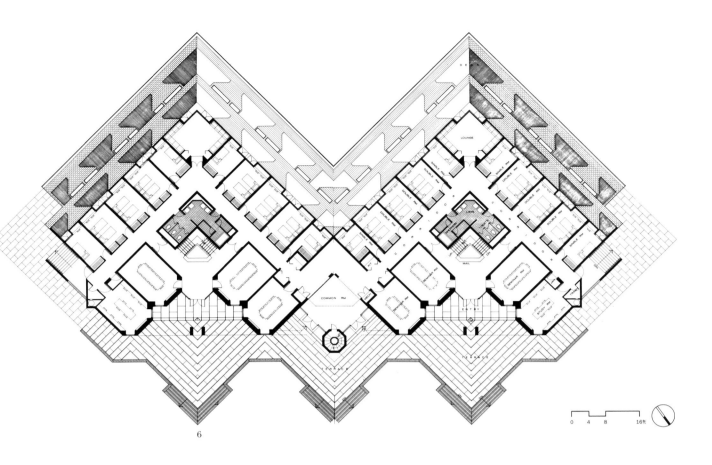

6

7

College Dormitory, Mount Vernon College   39

# Public Stable, Rock Creek Park

Design/Completion 1969/1972
Rock Creek Park
Washington, DC
US Department of the Interior/National Park Service
17,000 square feet
Wood frame
Painted board and batten siding; asphalt shingle
roof; earth and wood block floors

Located in a heavily wooded park,
the 220-foot long building was sited to
avoid extensive tree cutting and to follow
contour lines. The stable contains 20 box
stalls and 20 standing stalls with areas for
servicing, storage, grooming and public
viewing. Its basic form is a rectangle with
a four-way shed roof. In some places the
roof drops down to provide appropriate
ceiling heights for offices and other
ancillary spaces on the first floor,
while at other points the walls move up
and angle outward to provide entry for
large tractors and other mechanical
equipment. The wooden structure is
sheathed in wood board and batten
siding painted bright barn red and
trimmed in white.

The interior is configured as a practical
double-loaded corridor scheme with
a double-height center corridor. Natural
light and ventilation are brought into
the stable through clerestory windows.
The stable has since been demolished.

1

2

1 Office area
2 Entrance elevation towards east

# Saltonstall Barn

Design/Completion 1970/1972
Rappahannock County, Virginia
Mrs Patricia Saltonstall
1,800 square feet
Wood frame
Painted wood board and batten siding; wood
windows; painted standing seam metal roof;
earth floor

1   From the south
2   From the hill above

This stable complex is the gatehouse
to a small farm in the Blue Ridge
Mountains. The entrance drive to the
main house runs through the stable itself;
the angles of the walls picking up the
"S" bend of the road and allowing angled
parking. Other functions in the complex
include two box stalls, a workshop and
generator room, and a small apartment.

1

2

# Private Residence, Potomac, Maryland

Design/Completion 1972/1975
Potomac, Maryland
4,000 square feet
Wood and steel frame
Stained clear cedar siding; plywood;
wood and tile floors; built-up roof

The clients specifically requested
a "modern" house with the basic public
spaces (living, dining, library, etc.)
to be one large area divided by levels
or screening elements only. The kitchen
was to be located to have easy supervision
of the main part of the house. There were
to be separate areas for parents, children
and guests. The house is designed
as an "elaborated box".

The site is on three wooded acres, almost
completely private, sloping appreciably
to the east. The house faces due south,
while the first floor steps down to the east.
Overhangs shield the major openings
in the summer and trees break the early
and late low-angled sun in spring and fall
while allowing the winter sun to stream
in. The gray, wood-sheathed portion
of the house containing the private
functions bridges across the smaller,
white painted, stepped units of the
public spaces below.

1  Longitudinal section
2  Corner of breakfast area and deck
    off of dining room
3  Entrance portico

4　Main floor plan
5　Dining room towards sitting and living rooms

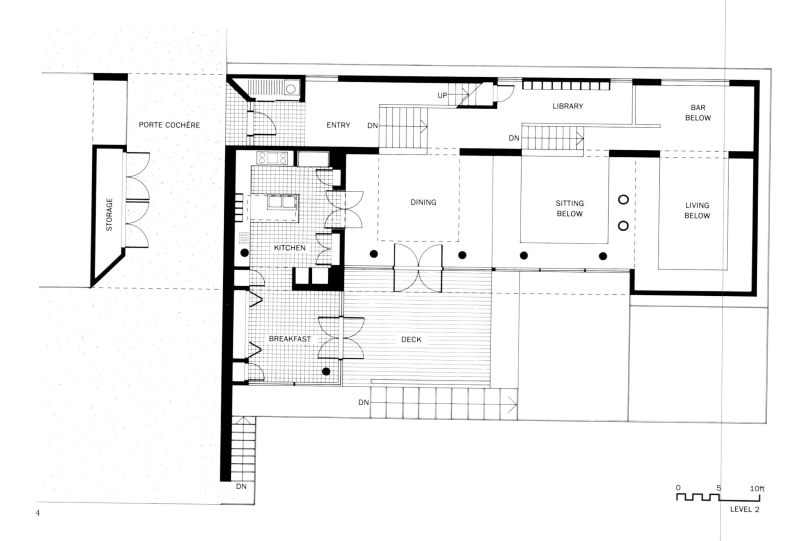

PORTE COCHÉRE

STORAGE

UP

ENTRY　DN

LIBRARY

BAR
BELOW

DN

KITCHEN

DINING

SITTING
BELOW

LIVING
BELOW

BREAKFAST

DECK

DN

DN

0　　5　　10ft

LEVEL 2

4

5

7

## National Bookstore, National Visitors' Center, Union Station

Design/Completion 1974/1976
Union Station
Washington, DC
US Department of the Interior/National Park Service/Parks and History Association
6,000 square feet
Existing structure
Plastic laminate-faced cases; carpeted plywood; brick and quarry tile floors

As part of the now removed National Visitors' Center, a new, large bookstore was installed in the old Washington Union Station. The room in which it was located was once a restaurant, measuring 60 feet by 100 feet in plan and 30 feet high, with a grid of fifteen large skylights in the ceiling. Sixteen pairs of heroically scaled Ionic columns line the walls, aligning with the skylights. The room itself was painted several shades of white and off-white. Virtual indestructibility and easy visual supervision were prime criteria for the new bookstore.

The bookstore was conceived as four layers of space, a succession of rooms within rooms. Three low enclosures—for desk, seating and children's books—form the innermost. They are bounded by two higher rows of bookcases. The room itself is the last enclosure. The stepping up also provides the required visual supervision from the desk. All of the elements of the bookstore align with the skylights, ceiling grid and paired columns of the room.

1

2

1  Entrance portico
2  Outside range of bookcases
3  Plan
4  From the entrance

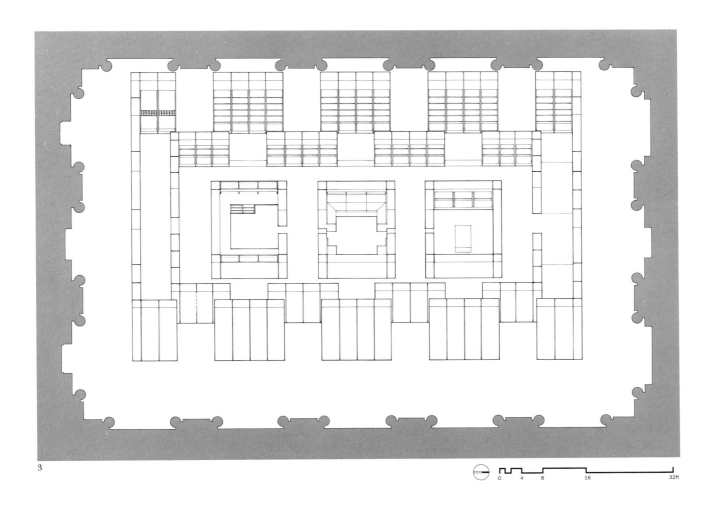

3

4

# National Permanent Building

Design/Completion 1974/1977
1775 Pennsylvania Avenue, NW
Washington, DC
The Lenkin Company, Bethesda, Maryland
240,000 square feet (including parking)
Reinforced concrete frame with flat slabs
Painted architectural concrete; painted metal ductwork;
membrane roof; fixed glazing; flagstone walls and floors;
steel grating sunscreens

The scale, gray and black color, and degree of forcefulness of the National Permanent Building were tailored to its prominent location on a triangular Pennsylvania Avenue site located two blocks from the White House. Intended as "a relatively tame foreground structure", it can be seen for over a mile up the Avenue to the west.

The eight-story building is defined by an external framework of round concrete columns which narrow as they rise to carry lighter loads, and by round air-conditioning ducts which narrow as they descend to carry lighter cooling loads. The scheme adheres to the modernist dictum of expressing function, while taking initial steps towards historicism by alluding to the nearby Old Executive Office Building with its multitude of exterior columns. Darkly tinted and inset—hence shaded—glazing on the west and south is a response to the energy mandates and available technologies of the 1970s.

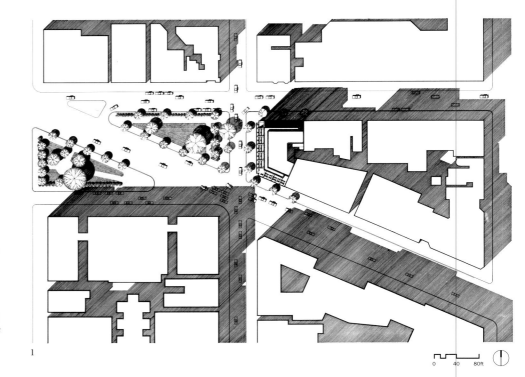

1

0    40    80ft

2

1  Site plan
2  The building from Pennsylvania Avenue
   looking east
3  Pennsylvania Avenue facade

3

4 West elevation on the park
5 Twelfth floor plan
6 Detail of south-west corner

4

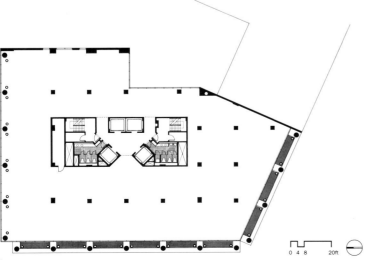

5

0 4 8    20ft

National Permanent Building   53

# National Humanities Center

Design/Completion 1976/1978
Triangle Research Park
Raleigh, North Carolina
Triangle University Center for Advanced
Studies Inc.
30,000 square feet
Brick bearing wall and steel frame
Painted brick; aluminum and steel skylights with
variably transmissive mirrored insulating glass;
brick paving

This center, conceived as an institute
for advanced studies in the humanities
by the American Academy of Arts and
Sciences, was intended as a sanctuary,
study center and meeting place
for recognized and promising scholars.
"It was to be elegant but not rich, spartan
but not institutional," as Nory Miller
wrote in *Architecture* magazine.

The low-lying building has been tucked
into its 15-acre wooded site, against which
its white brick and dark glass elevations
create a deliberate contrast. The center
has a rambling plan comprising individual
studies on two floors, conference rooms,
offices, a library and service areas.
These are organized around a large
central commons and lounge area.
All spaces are woven together by
transparent, gabled corridors along
which are lounges intended to foster
informal contact. Major spaces are
topped with canted skylights.

Interior materials and colors echo those
of the exterior—exposed red brick floors,
white painted brick walls and reflective
glass skylights.

1

1  Site plan
2  First floor plan
3  Center from entrance drive

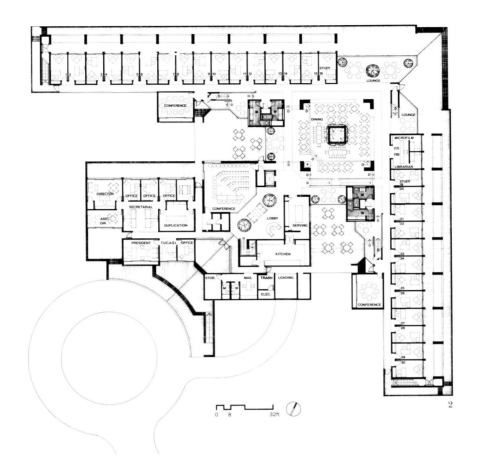

2

3

4

5

6

7

8

9 Bridge at refectory
10 Circulation area with lounge

9

# Immanuel Presbyterian Church

Design/Completion 1978/1980
888 Dolley Madison Boulevard
McLean, Virginia
Immanuel Presbyterian Church
4,500 square feet
Wood frame
Painted plywood with battens; custom and
conventional wood windows; asphalt shingle
roof; brick fireplace

1   Site plan
2   Building from the south-east
3   Building from the south-west

This church is actually a large addition
connected to a neo-colonial suburban
house (formerly used as the church)
located on a rolling, partially wooded six-
acre site. The church's main spaces—its
sanctuary, fellowship hall, school and
entry—were moved from the house to
the new building, which resembles an
abstracted barn with clustered dormers.
The new church runs parallel to the
existing house to which it is connected
via a "U"-shaped arcade, tying the entire
complex together. The arcade also creates
a courtyard focused on two mature linden
trees.

Dominating the addition's courtyard
facade is a mullioned and gabled double-
height window wall bisected by a chimney.
Above the glazed wall are dormers
admitting natural light to the rear of the
sanctuary. The building's south elevation,
by contrast, is largely windowless. It is
given visual interest through the use of
setbacks and more of the high dormers.
The sanctuary connects to the fellowship
hall via an interior mullioned window wall.

1

2

62

4 Ground level plan
5 Sanctuary
6 Sanctuary towards altar

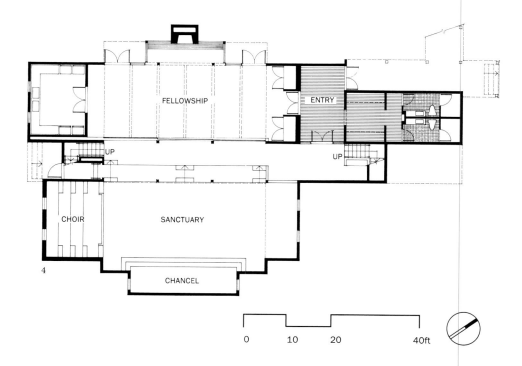

FELLOWSHIP

ENTRY

UP

UP

CHOIR

SANCTUARY

4

CHANCEL

0    10    20         40ft

5

6

7

8

9

10

# Remodeling and Addition, Washington, DC

Design/Completion 1978/1981
Washington, DC
1,800 square feet
Wood and steel frame
Wood; fieldstone; stucco; slate roof;
clay tile and wood floors

Except for the size and character
of the house, this would be a typical
addition and remodeling for a growing
family. The program called for an
enlarged kitchen, a new family room,
a second floor bedroom, a deck and
a new swimming pool.

The intent of the design was to blend
with and be sympathetic to the character
of the house while still maintaining some
level of abstraction.

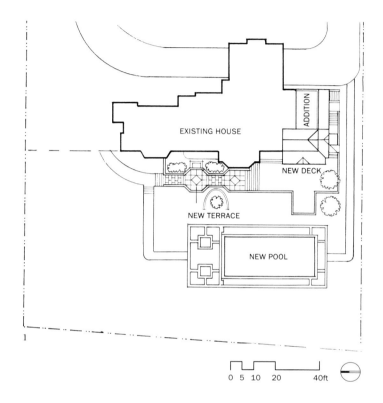

1   Site plan
2   Additions on right with new deck and pool
3   New swimming pool and deck with house beyond

3

4　First floor plan
5　Corner of family room

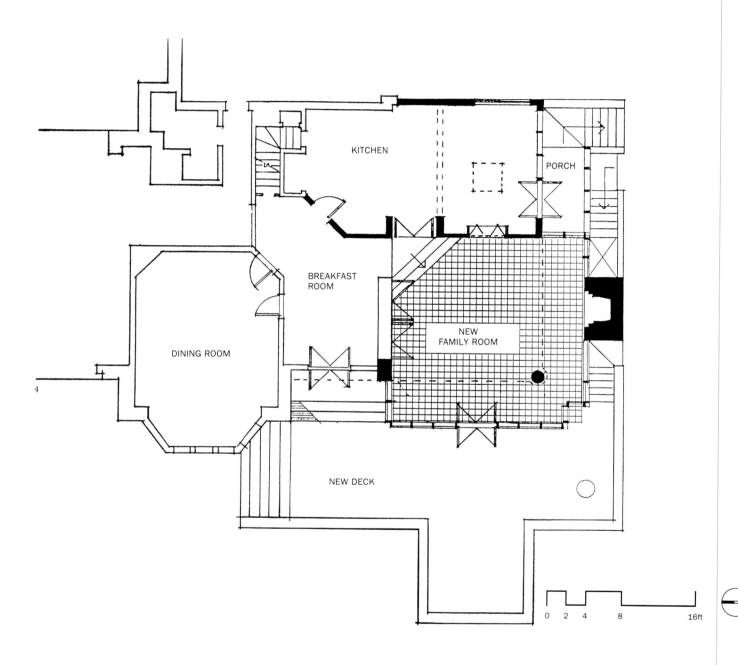

KITCHEN

PORCH

BREAKFAST
ROOM

NEW
FAMILY ROOM

DINING ROOM

4

NEW DECK

0  2  4     8            16ft

5

# 4250 Connecticut Avenue, NW

Design/Completion 1980/1983
Washington, DC
The Prudential Insurance Company of America
Newark, New Jersey
391,000 square feet (including parking)
Reinforced concrete frame and flat slab
Brick on CMU back-up; standard curtain wall
with three colors of glass; tile floors; exterior
precast paving

Because this speculative office building
with ground level storefronts is situated
at subway and bus stops, the design had
to accommodate a bus station at grade
and a basement automotive "kiss and ride"
drop-off. The building's unadorned,
modern-style and businesslike north and
rear elevations give access to two levels
of underground parking.

The building's street elevation of striped
tan and rust-colored brick is designed
in a neo-Art Deco idiom to recall nearby
buildings along Connecticut Avenue.
The complex contains two stories
of retail space and five floors of offices.
The low-lying, seven-story facade facing
the avenue defers not only to small,
neighboring 1920s buildings, but also
to the adjacent low-rise modernist
University of the District of Columbia.
The architects bent the building at its
center to align its southern half with the
adjoining university building, and to break
down its great length. Setbacks further
lessen its bulk. To differentiate the
building's volumes, the architects carved
out an oblong, meandering central
courtyard separating a foreground from
a background mass.

1

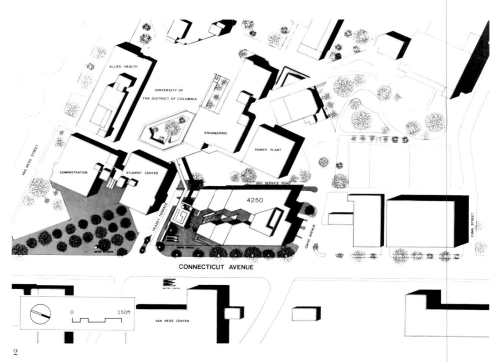

2

1 Entrance to courtyard
2 Site plan
3 Connecticut Avenue facade with University
of the District of Columbia beyond

3

# Folger Shakespeare Library and Addition

Design/Completion 1976/1983; completed in three stages
201 East Capitol Street, SE
Washington, DC
Trustees of Amherst College
Amherst, Massachusetts
30,000 square foot addition
79,000 square foot remodeling and renovation
Addition: steel frame with metal deck
Addition: steel studs with marble cladding; plaster; brown coat
plaster; wood and carpet floors; oak millwork; membrane roof

Renovations and additions to Paul Cret's 1920s stripped classical library, housing the foremost collection of Shakespearean material in the world, progressed over a period of seven years in three stages. First, new stacks were tucked into two underground levels at the rear of the building. Next, former interior stack areas became office space, the existing office and service spaces were remodeled and the entire building was air-conditioned. The final phase consisted of adding a new reading room and a "treasure room" leading into the vaults containing the Folger's rare book collection.

The new reading room is located over an earlier, one-story addition which was structurally unable to support any additional load. As a result, the new room had to be suspended on inverted "L"-shaped steel frames bearing on the outside on the new underground stacks and on the inside on the existing Cret building. This frame, painted white, is expressed as an exoskeleton for the marble-clad

*Continued*

1

2

1   The existing building
2   Rear of library before addition
3   Exterior of the addition looking towards
    the Library of Congress

74

3

volume of the reading room. The fluted marble slabs applied to the sides of the steel columns echo Cret's fluted pilasters on the opposite side. The stepping of the wall at the bays mimics the in-stepped entrances to the library.

The dimensions of the new three-part reading room are similar to those of the existing reading room, but as requested by the client, the new is light and airy while the old is dark and baronial in its grandeur. The addition's main space consists of a long, white rectangular volume topped by a barrel-vaulted ceiling which admits natural light through a central opening and narrow clerestories along the sides. At each end of this room are apse-like rounded sections, again lit around their perimeter. Arches are edged in false stonework, made of plaster. The room is used as a picture gallery for the library's extensive collection of Shakespeare-related paintings. The historic sources for the new reading room include Boullée's proposed Bibliothéque Nationale and Robert Adams' library at Kenwood House.

4

5

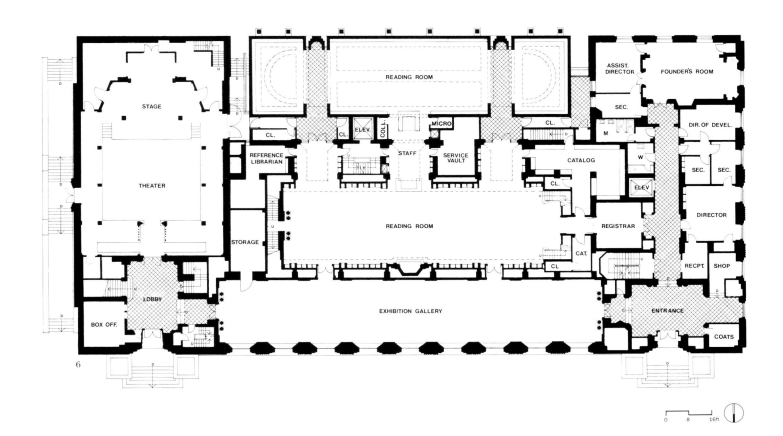

6

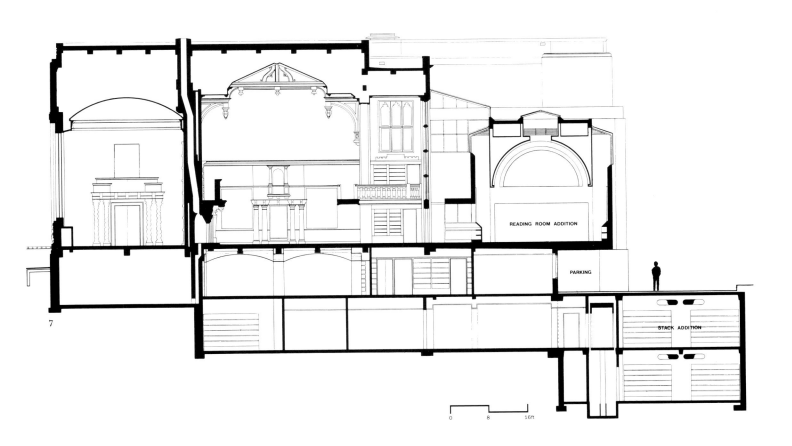

7

8   Treasure room
9   Existing reading room
10  New shop
11  Treasure (display) room with vault door leading
     to underground stacks and vaults

8

9

10

11

12

13

14 Vaults and arches in new reading room
15 Underside of vault, apex and skylights in new
   reading room

15

16 Detail of vault and end apse
17 New reading room
18 New reading room towards service desk
19 Niche and new architect-designed table

17

18

19

20  New reading room
21  Passage and apse in new reading room

20

# Foster House

Design/Completion 1981/1983
1001 Crest Lane
McLean, Virginia
Mr and Mrs P. Wesley Foster, Jr
6,000 square feet
Wood frame
Painted redwood clapboard siding;
painted standing seam metal roof;
custom and conventional wood windows;
wood floors; dry stone retaining walls

Located on a heavily wooded suburban
lot just north of Washington along
the Potomac River, the Foster House
is composed in the manner of a traditional
"railroad" plan farmhouse. The long,
wood frame dwelling consists of three
attached "little houses" that, in the past,
would have been built incrementally as
a family grew. This massing accommodates
the narrow, sloping site and the client's
request for a two-story house with
different, distinct living areas at ground
level. The dollhouse-like scale is the
result of the purposely overscaled and
unadorned windows, dormers and doors.

This character is extended within.
The top-lit entrance, one half story above
grade, serves as a stopping place between
upper-story twin bedrooms, lower-story
guest area, and the adjoining second little
house, which contains formal living and
dining areas suffused with natural light.
This leads to the dwelling's third element
containing an informal family room. A
porch, overlooking the Potomac River to
the east, runs the length of this room.

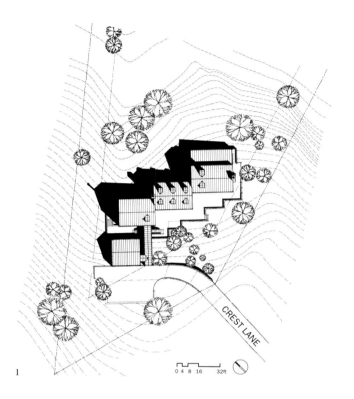

1

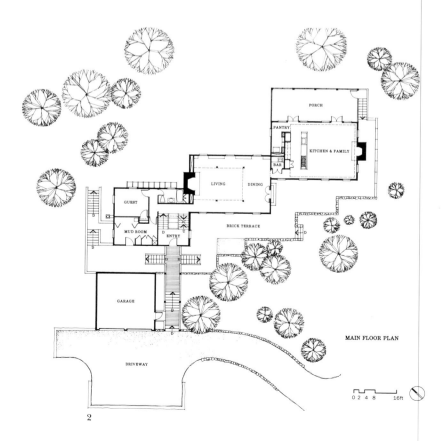

MAIN FLOOR PLAN

2

1 Site plan
2 Main floor plan
3 The house from the south with the entrance
   bridge on the left
4 The house from the south-east end with the
   kitchen and family room wing in the foreground

3

4

# United States Embassy Office Building, Kuala Lumpur

Design/Completion 1978/1983
Jalan Pekelling
Kuala Lumpur, Malaysia
US Department of State
80,000 square feet
Reinforced concrete frame with brick infill
"Shanghai" plaster; clay tile roof; enameled
steel sash; wire glass; tile floors

This United States chancery is essentially
an "H"-shaped complex, stratified
vertically. The most security-sensitive
areas—communications and the
ambassador's office, for example—are
on the upper floors and to the rear
of the building. Public areas, meanwhile,
are limited to the first floor, where visitors
are screened in a central lobby, sent left
to the consular section, right to the
cultural section, and straight ahead
to the embassy officials' offices.

The building has a poured-in-place
concrete frame with brick infill walls
covered with "Shanghai" plaster,
a material common in the area. To shade
the windows, protect them from torrential
rains, and give the building local flavor,
the architects added covered verandahs,
wide overhanging eaves, balustrades,
exterior stairways, tiled roofs, and lattice-
covered openings. The complex's largest

*Continued*

1

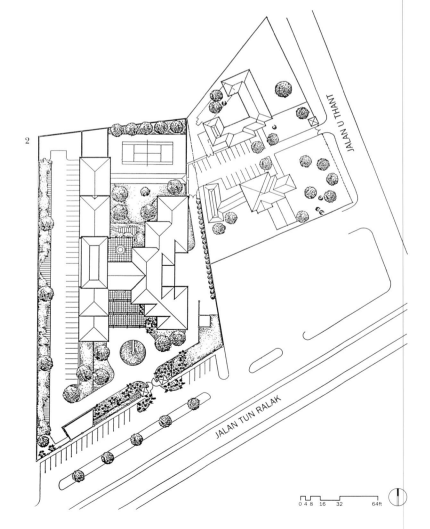

2

1  Entrance with marine guard stations
2  Site plan
3  Entry level plan
4  The entrance at night

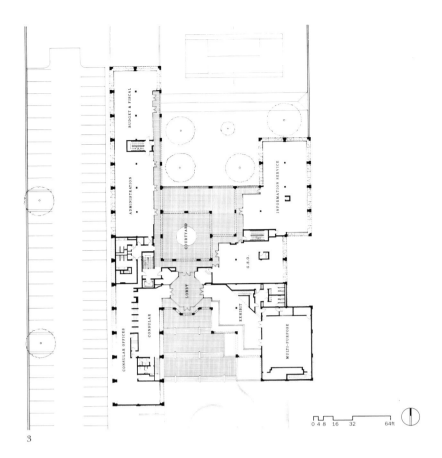

3

4

section—the embassy offices—were placed on the northern, commercial side of the site, and the building was stepped down to the south to take advantage of prevailing breezes and create a more residential scale. For security reasons, no exterior windows were permitted within 16 feet of the ground. The interiors are, therefore, organized around a series of courtyards on several levels.

It is interesting to note that this building created something of a controversy among the local Malaysian architects, some of whom believed that the embassy should have been an "international style" modern building, not, as they saw it, a throwback to colonialism and traditional Malaysian architecture.

5

6

5   Courtyard on the east side
6   Courtyard looking south
7   Balconies at second floor

7

# Apex Building

Design/Completion 1982/1984
7th Street and Pennsylvania Avenue, NW
Washington, DC
Historic Central Bank Redevelopment Group
Washington, DC
45,000 square feet
Reinforced concrete frame with flat slabs
Brick; stucco; wood windows; marble lobby floors

Poised halfway between the White House and the Capitol, this project was the first privately-funded restoration on Pennsylvania Avenue in recent years. Three historically significant pre-Civil War structures were revived and enhanced. The towered structure terminating the complex on the west was designed by A.B. Mullet, architect of the Old Executive Office Building. The two adjoining buildings on the east once housed the studio of famed Civil War photographer Matthew Brady.

The 19th century buildings were refurbished. A mid-block infill structure was inserted, closing the existing gap in the row, and missing storefronts were restored, using faded photographs as references throughout the work. The architects also added a sixth floor office penthouse. As completed for Sears, Roebuck and Company, the Apex Building comprises 45,000 square feet of office space.

The new work, using materials, proportions, and style derived from the existing work, unifies the entire group. Hartman-Cox was responsible for the exterior design only. John Milner Associates was the historic preservation consultant.

1

2

94

1   Pennsylvania Avenue facade before construction
2   Apex Building from G Street and Pennsylvania Avenue
3   Pennsylvania Avenue facade after construction
4   First floor plan

3

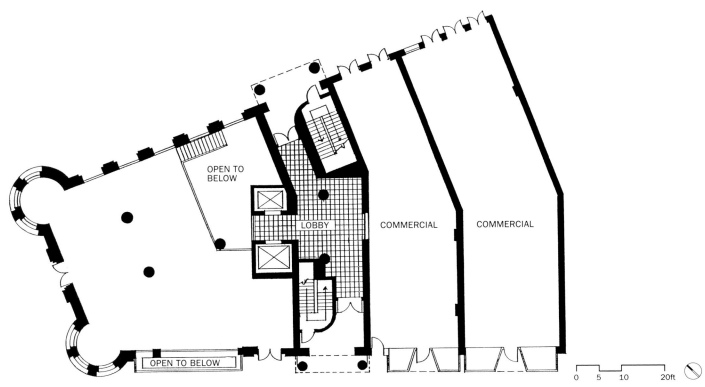

OPEN TO BELOW

OPEN TO BELOW

LOBBY

COMMERCIAL

COMMERCIAL

0   5   10      20ft

4

## Commerce Place

Design 1985; not constructed
Baltimore, Maryland
The Harlan Company
New York, New York
659,000 square feet
Reinforced concrete frame with flat slabs
Dark gray granite facing on CMU; aluminum sash

Commerce Place was to have included
a 55 foot high, top-lit "galleria",
incorporating elements from the facade
of a historic banking institution as the
entrance for the high-rise office tower.
The axis of the galleria would have
extended a major downtown street
and formed the principal entrance
to the complex. The facades of the
historic bank were to be re-erected along
its two long sides. The office tower was
to rise 28 stories above the north portion
of the site and step in to provide three
different floor sizes.

The base of the building was scaled
to relate to the entrances and storefronts
in the immediate neighborhood.
A secondary, higher base element rose
out of this to relate, in turn, to nearby
mid-rise buildings. The shaft and upper
portion of the tower were intended
to reflect a number of typical Baltimore
office building characteristics: recessed
upper floors and large-scale elements
at the top; contrasting use of stone
and curtain wall infill; and the frequent
use of balconies.

1

2

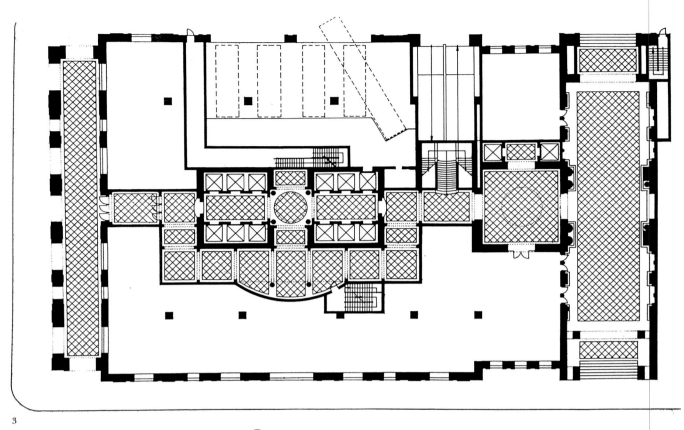

3

0   8   16      32ft

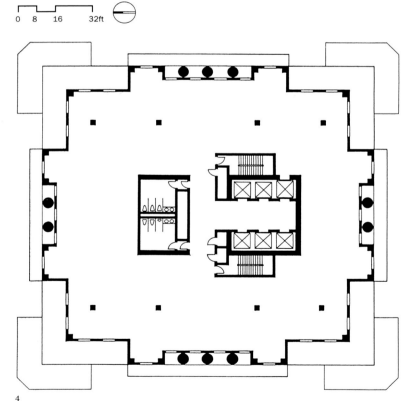

4

5

6 Section through gallery
7 Upper stories
8 Down Redwood Street towards gallery entrance
9 Baltimore Street elevation

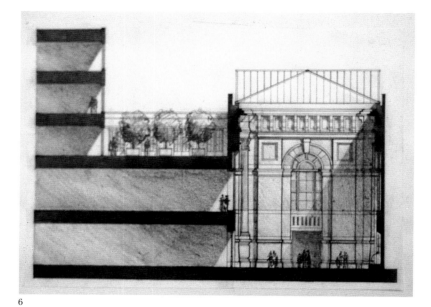

6

7

8

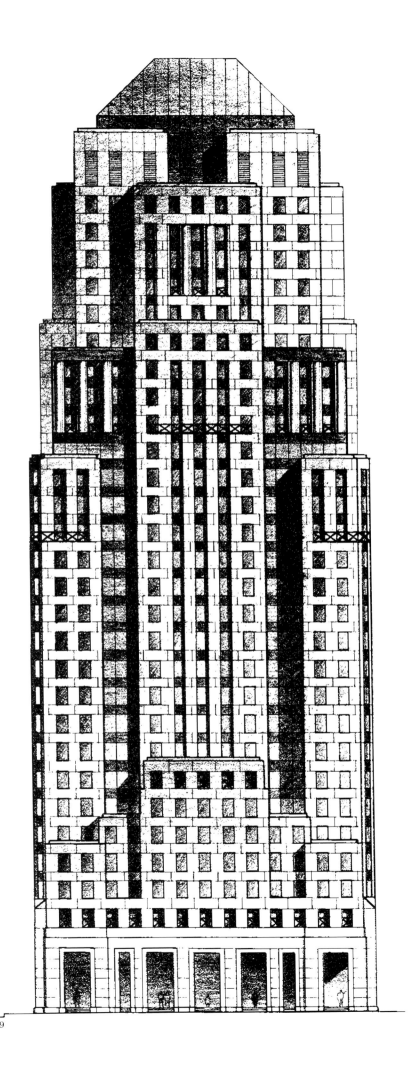

9

# Headquarters for the H.E. Butt Grocery Company

Design/Completion 1981/1985
646 South Main Avenue
San Antonio, Texas
H.E. Butt Grocery Company
180,000 square feet
Reinforced concrete and steel frame
Stucco on CMU; cast stone; wood railings;
custom steel windows; unpainted standing
seam metal and membrane roofs; native buff
limestone and exposed aggregate paving

This project involved the conversion
of an old United States Army arsenal
complex into the corporate headquarters
of the major independent grocery
company of south Texas.

The site consists of approximately 10 acres
along the San Antonio Riverwalk, across
from a historic residential area that is
listed on the National Register of Historic
Places. The site contained a mix of largely
nondescript industrial buildings located
without regard for their spatial
relationships and in a state of total
disrepair. Three buildings—the two small
buildings in the new courtyard (the Old
Arsenal and the Stable) and the long,
four-story warehouse to the south—have
been restored. By selective demolition,
heavy remodeling and major additions
to the other existing buildings, and by the
addition of an arcade and the new three-
story building to the north, a new
courtyard complex has been formed.
The work is about 75 per cent new.

*Continued*

1

2

1 The completed complex from the east
2 The Stable before restoration
3 Site plan after completion

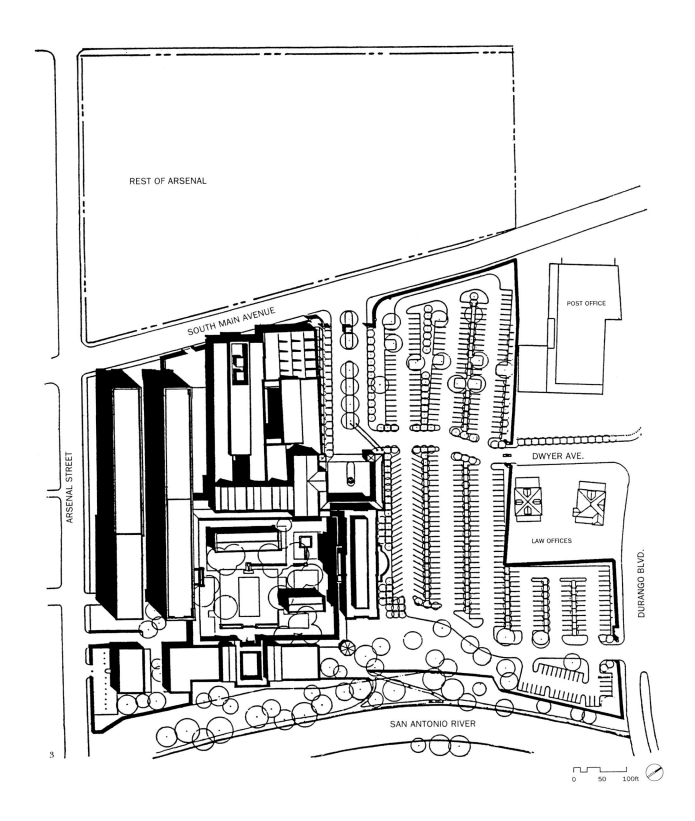

REST OF ARSENAL

SOUTH MAIN AVENUE

ARSENAL STREET

POST OFFICE

DWYER AVE.

LAW OFFICES

DURANGO BLVD.

SAN ANTONIO RIVER

3

0    50    100ft

Headquarters for the H.E. Butt Grocery Company    103

The stucco walls match those of the existing warehouse and contrast with the limestone of the Stable and the Arsenal. The new pediments reflect the shape of those on the Arsenal and the Stable and the capitals of the columns in the entrance use a motif found on an existing building. The elements along the river have been kept low and relatively small to reflect the residential scale opposite.

The intent in the design of the new work has been to develop an architectural character responsive to the utilitarian character of existing buildings, the rich and unique architecture of the region, and the requirements of a corporate headquarters. The associated architect was Chumney/Urrutiae of San Antonio. Raiford Stripling was the historic preservation consultant.

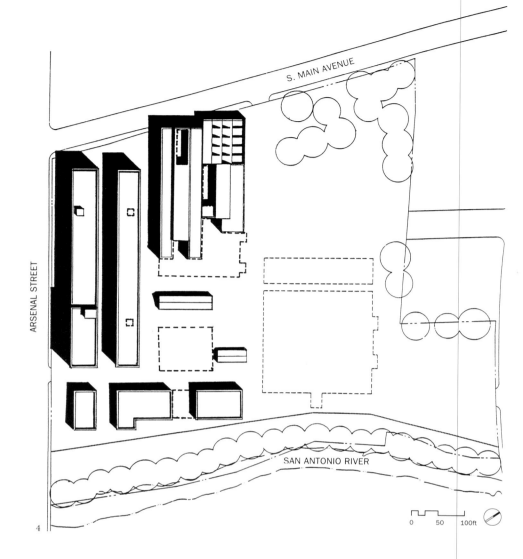

6

7

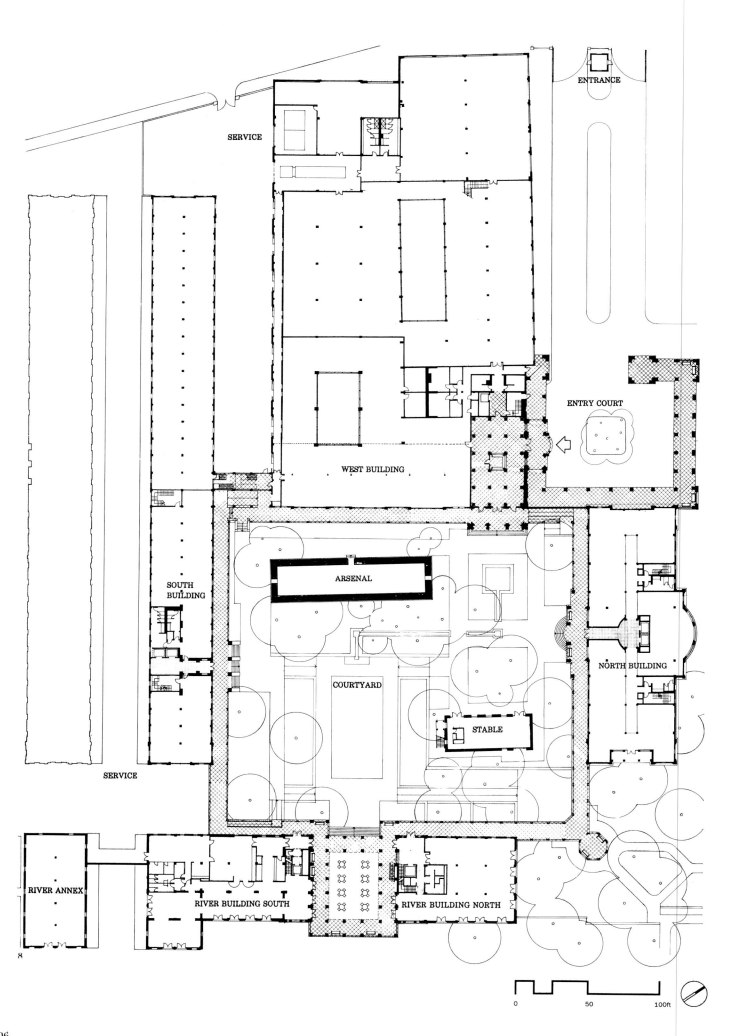

ENTRANCE

SERVICE

ENTRY COURT

WEST BUILDING

SOUTH
BUILDING

ARSENAL

NORTH BUILDING

SERVICE

COURTYARD

STABLE

RIVER ANNEX

RIVER BUILDING SOUTH

RIVER BUILDING NORTH

8

0    50    100ft

9

10

11

12

13

11 The complex from across the San Antonio River
   looking towards downtown
12 The overlook off of the arcade
   in the north-east corner
13 The north-east corner of the courtyard

14

15

14 The administration or north building
   from the west or entrance building
15 The restored Stable building from
   the courtyard entrance
16 Looking west from the north building
17 Entrance lobby

16

17

18

19

20

# 1001 Pennsylvania Avenue, NW

Design/Completion 1979/1986
Washington, DC
Cadillac Fairview Urban Development Inc.
Dallas, Texas
1,200,000 square feet (including parking)
Reinforced concrete flat slab
Variegated Indiana limestone; brick;
white Carrara and Verdi St Nicholas marble; painted faux marble
on dry wall; custom aluminum storefronts with bronze trim;
aluminum windows with clear insulating glass; membrane roof

Located where federal and commercial
Washington meet, the block-sized retail
and office building between 10th Street
and 11th Street on the north side
of Pennsylvania Avenue is at once a
monumental building and an accretion
of new and restored existing structures.
On the avenue side, where it faces the
1920s Beaux-Arts buildings that comprise
the Federal Triangle, 1001 Pennsylvania
presents a rectangular, symmetrical facade
with vertical modulation, a tall rusticated
base, and a projecting tenth story and
heavy cornice line, all of which reiterate
elements of nearby buildings. Its other
three elevations—facing the 1890s
Evening Star Building to the west, the
1960s FBI Building to the east, and the old
commercial downtown core to the north—
are composed in three horizontal layers.
These rise in height as they recede, while
becoming less distinct in their articulation
and detailing.

*Continued*

1

1   Detail on Tenth Street with United States Storage
    Building facade
2   Pennsylvania Avenue facade
3   The south-west corner on Pennsylvania Avenue

2

3

The attempt on these sides is to create the appearance of a streetscape rather than that of a monolithic building, and thereby reduce the apparent bulk of the building.

Embedded in the side and rear elevations are five existing downtown facades which have been refurbished by the architects. On the north-west corner, two pairs of four-story brick structures have been incorporated into the new construction. On the Tenth Street side, the monumental sandstone and brick United States Storage Building of 1909 has been retained at the center of the new block.

In the manner of 19th-century European arcades, the four surrounding streets extend into the building via interior concourses which intersect at a central, seven-story, octagonal lobby rotunda.

The associated architect was Smith, Segreti, Tepper Architects & Planners, PC. Oehrlein and Associates was the historic preservation consultant.

4

5

7 Building directory
8 Ground floor plan
9 The rotunda

7

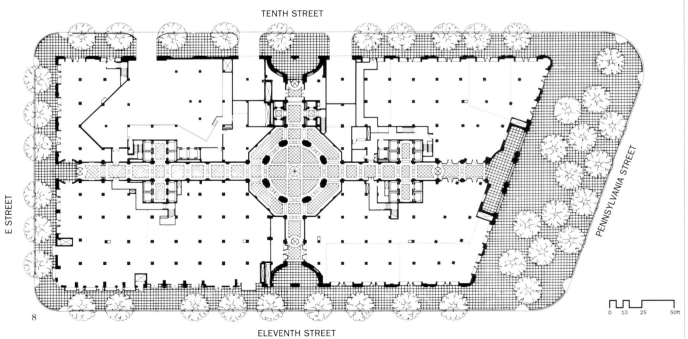

TENTH STREET

E STREET

PENNSYLVANIA STREET

8

ELEVENTH STREET

0  10  25      50ft

9

10  South concourse
11  Rotunda looking up

10

12  Elevator cab
13  Marble elevator door jam

12

13

# Gallery Row

Design/Completion 1983/1986
Seventh and D Streets, NW
Washington, DC
Carly Capital Group
Washington, DC
60,000 square feet
Reinforced concrete frame with flat slabs
Brick; architectural precast concrete; wood windows; marble

While this complex of businesses and shops was once one of the old downtown's busiest sections, in recent years it had become a rundown art corridor. Gallery Row's three floors of office space above street-oriented galleries were rebuilt behind one new and five restored facades. These facades had been so badly damaged by fire, water and subway construction as to require dismantling and rebuilding on a new concrete frame structure. The recreated storefronts are based on original or typical designs, some of which were hidden beneath later alterations and additions.

At the heart of the complex is a new infill building which houses the entry and core facilities. The new facade, built of precast concrete panels and columns, expresses a winding, monumental stair that connects the complex's non-aligned floors.

Oehrlein and Associates was the historic preservation consultant.

1

2

1  The existing conditions from the south-west
2  After restoration and the addition
3  Ground floor plan
4  The new stair between the two restored buildings

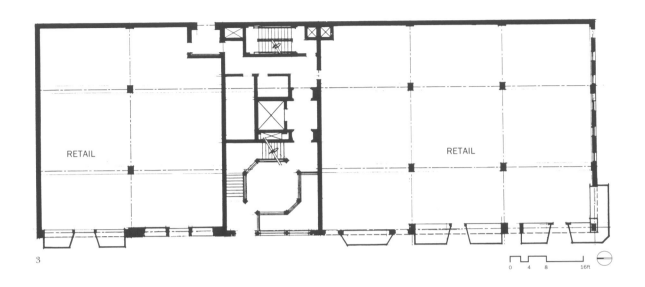

3

RETAIL

RETAIL

0  4  8    16ft

4

5

# Private Residence, Washington, DC

Design/Completion 1983/1986
Washington, DC
15,000 square feet
Wood frame
Wood clapboard; slate roof; brick foundation;
wood floors; soapstone paving

This large, new, single family house sits
on one of the highest sites in Washington,
overlooking both the District of Columbia
and Virginia. The clients requested
a relatively informal plan suitable
for entertaining large groups, and a house
reminiscent of a shingle style "cottage".
Site improvements include a swimming
pool and tennis court.

1

1   Front elevation
2   Front along porch
3   The long porch

2

Private Residence, Washington, DC 129

# St Patrick's Episcopal Church and Day School

Design/Completion 1981/1986
4700 Whitehaven Parkway, NW
Washington, DC
St Patrick's Episcopal Church
35,000 square feet
Masonry bearing wall and steel frame
Two colors of brick; painted metal standing seam
roof; aluminum windows; custom-milled wood
windows, painted; blue stone paving

This church was constructed adjacent to the parish's existing, stylistically modern day school in a residential neighborhood. The church was intended to appear old from the day it was completed and, in doing so, makes reference to several superb historic neo-gothic and neo-Romanesque churches in Washington. It is meant to look very much like a traditional Episcopal church. Because the church is surrounded by small-scale, traditional brick houses, the design is broken down into an abundance of small, gabled brick shapes.

The church, complete with campanile, is linked to the existing school by a new courtyard. The visitor enters both the church and the school through this courtyard, which also serves as a focus for the building's interior spaces.

In addition to the church, the interiors accommodate administrative offices, spaces for elementary and Sunday school use, a library, and a center for senior parishioners. The main church meeting room is an informal space with wooden floors.

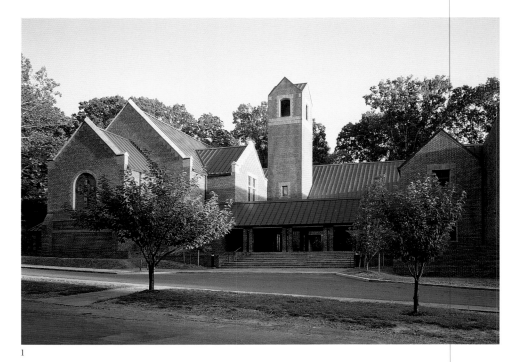

1

2

1   Sanctuary from the exterior
2   From the north-east
3   The church with existing school on the right
4   From the north-east; the sanctuary is on the
    near corner

3

4

5 Site plan
6 Entrance courtyard
7 Detail of brickwork and windows

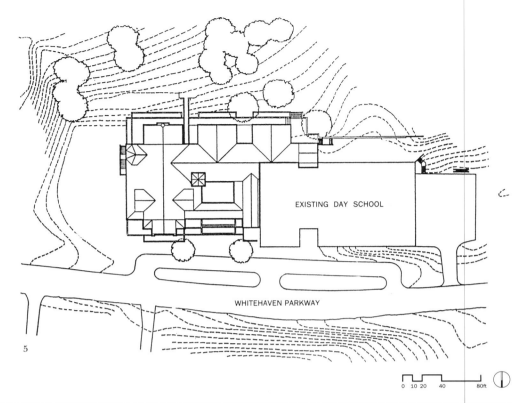

EXISTING DAY SCHOOL

WHITEHAVEN PARKWAY

5

0 10 20 40 80ft

6

7

8

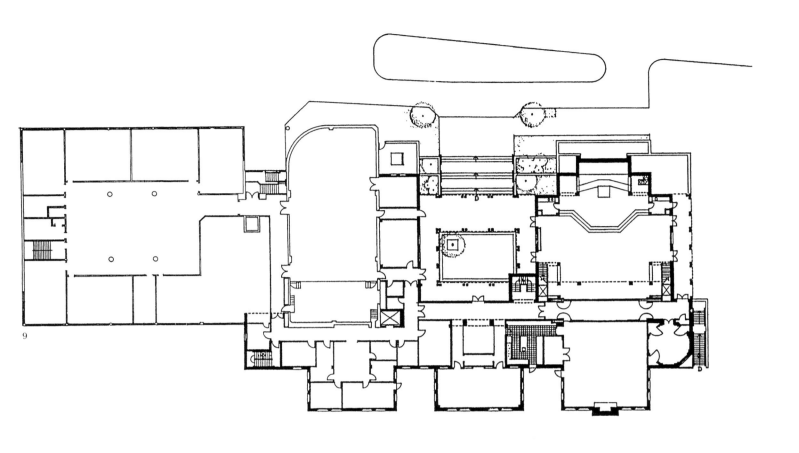

9

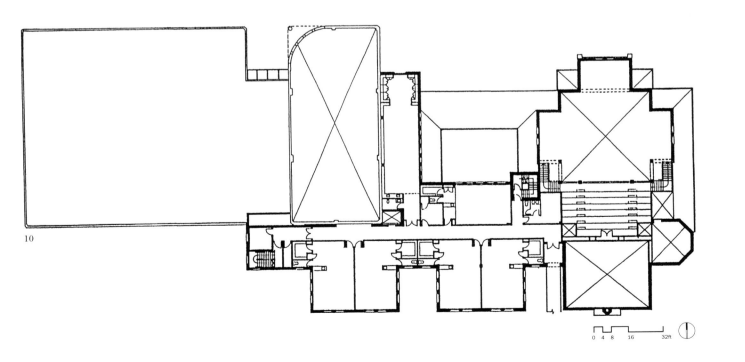

10

11

12

11 The rear of the sanctuary with parish hall beyond
12 The sanctuary
13 Chancel choir and organ

13

# Sumner School Complex

Design/Completion 1983/1986
1600 Block of M Street, NW
Washington, DC
17 M Associates
Washington, DC
350,000 square feet (including parking)
Reinforced concrete frame and flat slabs; edge beams
New and reused brick on CMU back-up; custom aluminum
curtain wall; slate and membrane roofs; architectural
precast concrete; marble walls and floors

The result of a design competition,
this ensemble comprises a diminutive
cityscape of two restored red brick schools
from the late 19th century that have been
converted to office use, a small addition
to one of them, and a new, "L"-shaped
curtain wall and masonry office building.

The complex begins at the corner of 17th
and M Streets with a restored historic
landmark, the Charles Sumner School of
1872 by Adolph Cluss. This was extended
with an addition almost indistinguishable
from the original building. Just east of the
Sumner School is the former Magruder
School, a building of little intrinsic
distinction which was retained for its
esthetic compatibility with the Sumner
School. The Magruder building was
disassembled and moved four feet to
accommodate parking underneath and
become the block's centerpiece. The two
schools were then connected via an 11-
story glazed background tower for which
new gabled brick entrance wings were
created. These flank the Magruder School

*Continued*

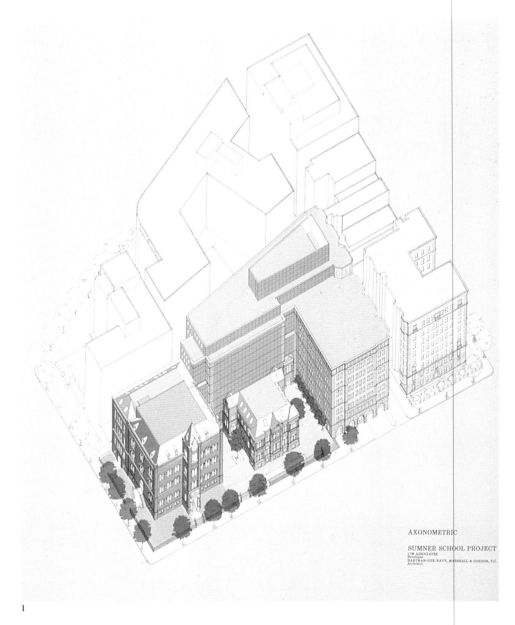

AXONOMETRIC

SUMNER SCHOOL PROJECT
17M ASSOCIATES
Developer
HARTMAN-COX-NAVY, MARSHALL & GORDON, P.C.
Architect

1

2

1  Axonometric of project
2  The project from the south-west corner
   after completion
3  The complex prior to restoration and the
   additions. Magruder School is hidden behind
   the trees on the right.

3

and emulate its style. Just east of the Magruder School, the tower steps forward, with its glazed facade replaced by masonry to blend with the adjacent landmark Jefferson Hotel of 1923, which terminates the block.

The entire complex centers on the courtyard of the National Geographic Society across M Street to the south, making a block in Washington unique in its urbanity and variety.

RTKL/The Ehrenkrantz Group were architects for the restoration of Sumner School. The associated architect was Navy Marshall & Gordon.

4

5

4 The restored Sumner School on the right side
with the office building addition behind

5 The complex from the south; Sumner School
is on the left and Magruder School is in the center

6 First floor plan

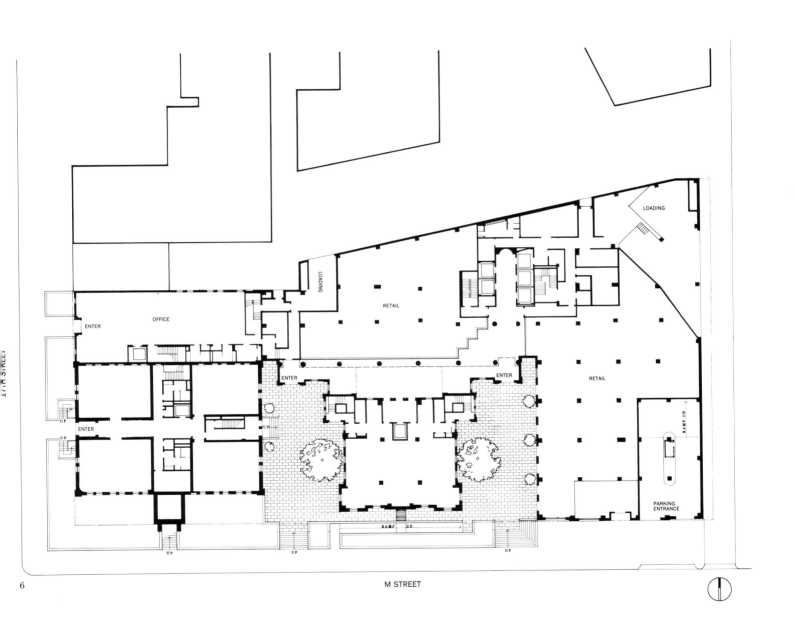

6

M STREET

7   The east entrance courtyard
8   Restored tower of Sumner School

8

9   One of the pair of new entrance towers
10  The new atrium behind Magruder School

9

# Corcoran Gallery of Art Office Building

Design 1985–1987; unbuilt to date
17th and New York Avenues, NW
Washington, DC
Corcoran Gallery of Art
186,000 square feet (including parking)
Concrete frame with flat slabs
Marble on CMU back-up; custom metal
windows; interior limestone; built-up roof

This seven-story office addition presents an almost seamless continuation of Ernest Flagg's justly acclaimed 1890s National Register museum and art school. The new roofline, cornice and belt courses all follow those of the Corcoran, and the addition's top two floors, rising above the adjacent Corcoran School, are set back at the same angle as the roof of the existing building. Elements of the existing building—including the doorway, windows, rusticated base, pilasters, capitals, cornice and metalwork—echo the existing building.

The new structure meets Flagg's with a four-story high, seven bay wide segment, followed by a six-story central pavilion, an echo of the Corcoran School of Art. The composition terminates with a cylindrical bay recalling the existing hemicycle at the corner of 17th Street and New York Avenue. The new addition is, however, intended to look like an office building, not a museum extension.

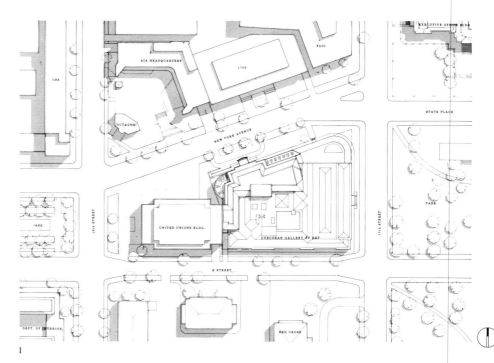

1

2

146

1 Site plan
2 The existing building from the intersection
3 The proposed addition

3

4   The existing site elevation
5   Proposed ground floor plan
6   Flagg's rendering of the front elevation
    of the Corcoran Gallery of Art
7   Model along New York Avenue

4

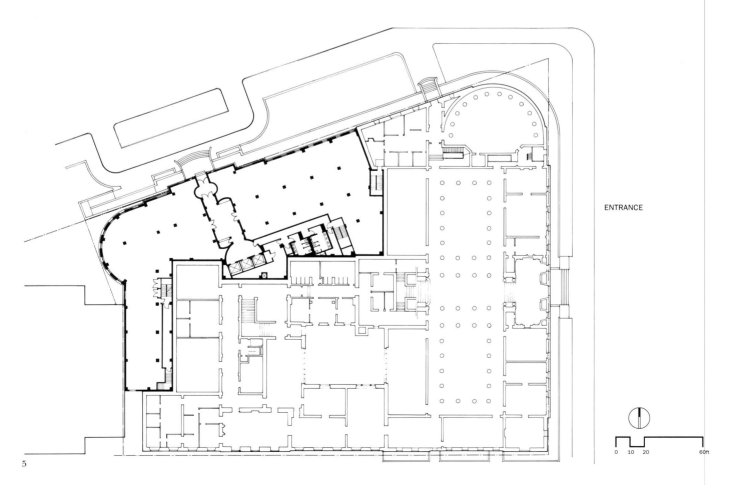

5

ENTRANCE

0  10  20                    60ft

6

7

# Monroe Hall, University of Virginia

Design/Completion 1984/1987
McIntire School of Commerce
University of Virginia
Charlottesville, Virginia
University of Virginia
35,000 square foot addition
Steel frame, metal deck with concrete slabs
Brick on CMU back-up; slate roof; slate floors;
custom wood sash and millwork

The McIntire School of Commerce is located on the older part of the University of Virginia campus. It is situated adjacent to Jefferson's lawn on McCormick Road, directly opposite the monumental Alderman Library, and is surrounded by colonial revival buildings.

The extension of 35,000 square feet of classroom and office space adds a fourth leg to the square "U" shape of the original building, transforming the footprint into a rectangular doughnut. On the north elevation, the monumental columns balance those of the Alderman Library and the five-part facade has the same basic configuration. For the addition's east side, the forms and proportions of the old building were replicated down to the 12-over-12 windows, which give high public rooms on the ground floor and offices with low arched windows above.

The interiors focus on a light-filled arcade bordering the central, newly landscaped courtyard. Classrooms are configured in a concentric "U"-shaped seating plan which creates good sightlines and accommodates maximum seating.

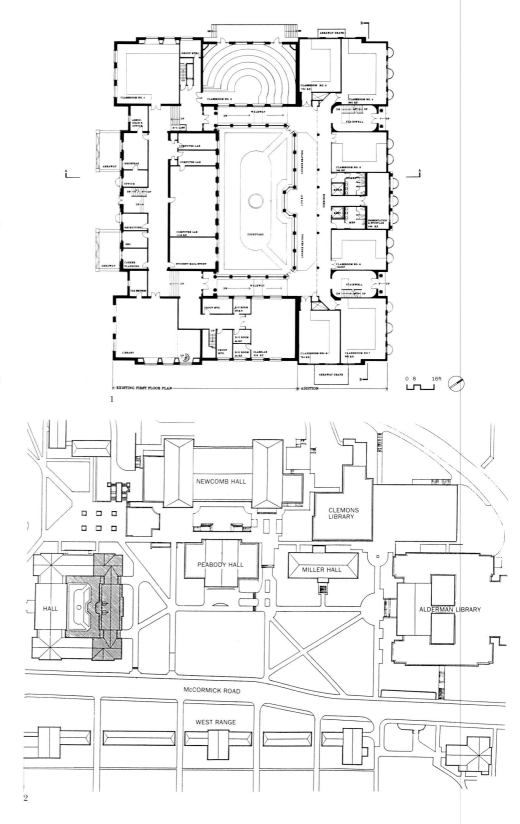

1

2

1    Ground floor plan
2    Site plan
3    South elevation of existing building
4    Monroe Hall before addition

3

4

6

7

8 Detail of addition
9 After the addition from the north
10 The new courtyard

Monroe Hall, University of Virginia    155

11 New corridor in addition
12 End of corridor with donor plaque

11

# Chrysler Museum

Design/Completion 1982/1989
Olney Road and Mowbray Arch
Norfolk, Virginia
Chrysler Museum
50,000 square feet new space
40,800 square feet remodeled space
Reinforced concrete frame
Variegated Old Gothic Indiana limestone;
Portland cement plaster; clay roof tiles;
heavy timber wood trusses in skylit courtyard;
marble and wood floors

The architects' charge was to improve the museum's exterior appearance, clarify its incomprehensible circulation, renovate 40,800 square feet of its exhibition space, and add 3,000 square feet for new galleries. The 1930s neo-Florentine Renaissance design of the Chrysler had been badly compromised by a pair of visually incompatible additions and the relocation of the entrance to the rear of the building away from the original, monumental entrance facade.

The main entrance was shifted back to the original location facing the Hague Canal, and the original arched entrance loggia, which had been bricked shut, was reopened. The architects balanced the entry elevation with a new wing of galleries and a second tower to the north, matching those to the south, and wrapped the new additions in limestone in the style of the original structure.

*Continued*

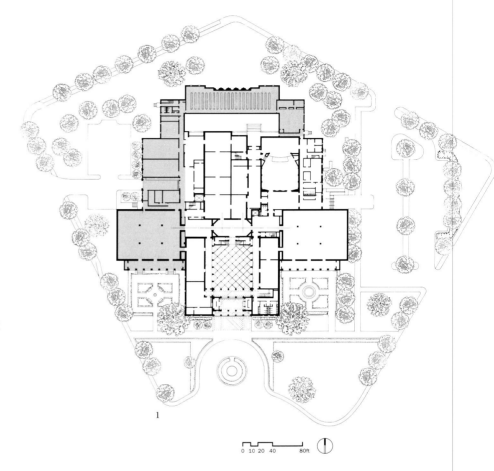

1

0 10 20 40    80ft

1   Ground floor plan
2   The museum from the west after the additions
3   East facade after additions

2

3

The central courtyard was covered with a skylight, its previously closed surrounding arcade was re-opened, and a cross axis created through the courtyard to the new galleries on the north. A new monumental stair gives access to the second floor galleries.

Finally, the architects concealed a 1974 brutalist addition with a new library wing. Within, moldings, cornices and baseboards, as well as cove lighting in the ceilings, were added.

4

4   Remodeled gallery
5   Enclosed court with new stairs, floor and skylight

5

6 Reopened arcade looking into covered courtyard
7 The new court

6

7

8

8   The court from the entry
9   The remodeled west facade with reopened doors
10  The east elevation before the additions
11  Detail of new wall

9

10

11

# Georgetown University Law Center Library

Design/Completion 1984/1989
600 New Jersey Avenue, NW
Washington, DC
Georgetown University
145,000 square feet
Reinforced concrete frame with flat slabs
Architectural precast concrete; terrazzo;
custom aluminum window grills; custom mahogany
millwork; carpeting; membrane roof

This full-block building accommodates
one of the largest law libraries in the
country and forms the first component
of a new complex which doubles the size
of the existing law center. The library
stands to the north of Edward Durrell
Stone's existing 1960s law center and
both complements and contrasts with it.
Like Stone's building, the new building
is placed on a podium and has a repetitive
ordering of facades. It also emulates
the Stone building in height and color.
In contrast to the Stone building,
the library holds the street line on three
sides and precast concrete was used
as exterior material instead of buff
poured-in-place concrete and buff-glazed
brick. Nor was Stone's trademark roof slab
cornice repeated.

*Continued*

1

1 The entrance and rotunda
2 The new law library across the closed
 street from the existing building
3 North elevation on Massachusetts Avenue

2

3

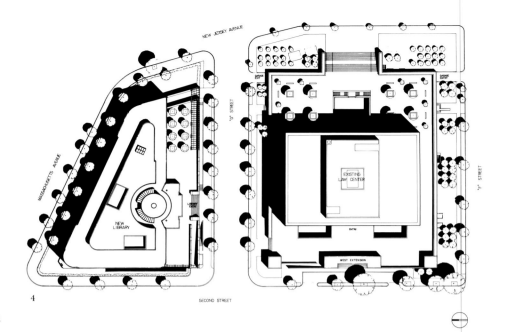

The building can accommodate up to 500,000 volumes and study seating for 1,200 students, combining flexible stack and reader spaces with a double height main reading room. The design recalls traditional university library reading rooms and the Folger Shakespeare Library, which the architects had earlier remodeled. The reading room is expressed on the exterior in the two-story windows facing north onto Massachusetts Avenue. The entry point of the building, around which all of the spaces are arranged, consists of a three-story atrium designed in the spirit of central, top-lit interior courts such as that found in Washington's Corcoran Gallery and, in particular, K.F. Schinkel's Altes Museum in Berlin.

4   Site plan
5   The north-west corner
6   The north-east corner with the Capitol beyond

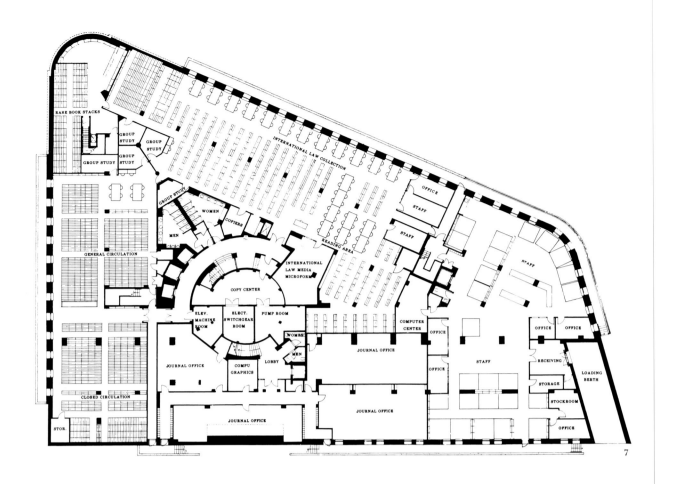

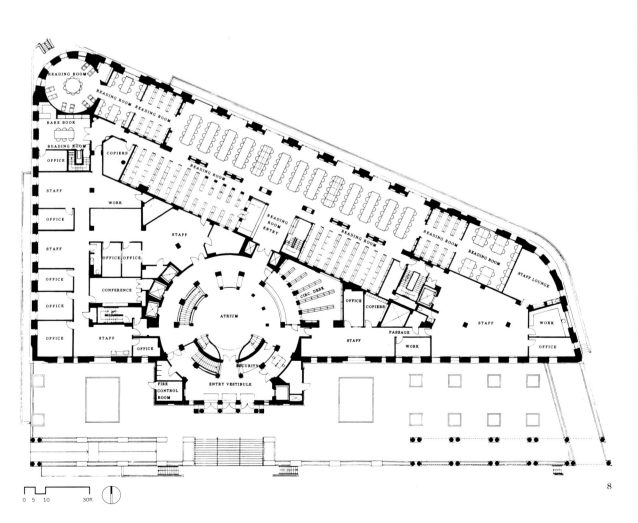

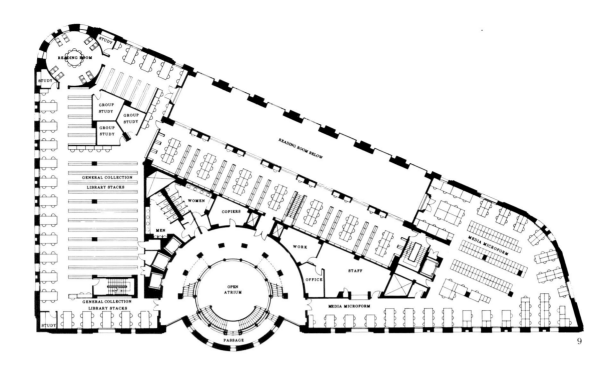

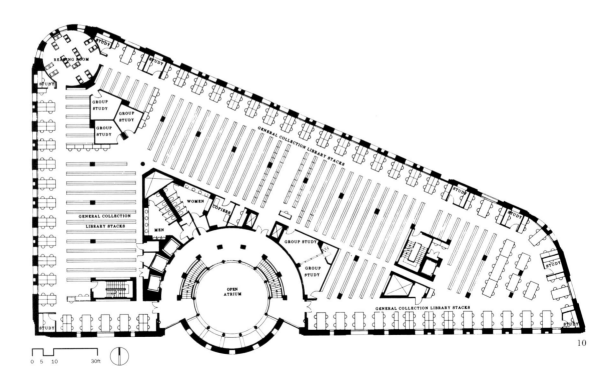

7 B1 level plan
8 First floor plan
9 Second floor plan
10 Third floor plan

11 The lounge over the atrium
12 Across the atrium towards the entrance
13 The atrium from the second floor

11

12

13

14

14  The reading room towards the balcony
15  The reading room from the balcony
16  The reading room

15

# Dumbarton Oaks Addition and Remodeling

Design/Completion 1985/1990
1703 32nd Street, NW
Washington, DC
Trustees of Harvard University
Cambridge, Massachusetts
10,000 square feet
Steel, limestone columns and reinforced concrete frame
Brick; Indiana limestone; plaster walls; vaulted plaster ceiling;
marble floors; custom mahogany trim and millwork; aluminum
and glass exterior skylight; frosted glass interior laylight
with wood muntins

Dumbarton Oaks museum and study center began in 1801 as a Federalist-style farmhouse, was Victorianized in the 19th century and expanded and refurbished in the 20th by Thomas T. Waterman and Philip Johnson, among other architects. In addition to adding a new, large display area, the new design improved security by separating research and staff areas from public spaces, enlarged the entry vestibule, clarified interior circulation, and added new underground mechanical areas, storage, and library stacks. None of the alterations changed the exterior appearance of Dumbarton Oaks.

The new gallery fits into a previously inaccessible outdoor courtyard bordered by an overstuffed Byzantine gallery, two hallways, and McKim, Mead and White's renowned 1929 music room, which provided cues for the new room. The new gallery is surrounded on three sides by a colonnaded ambulatory, whose paired

*Continued*

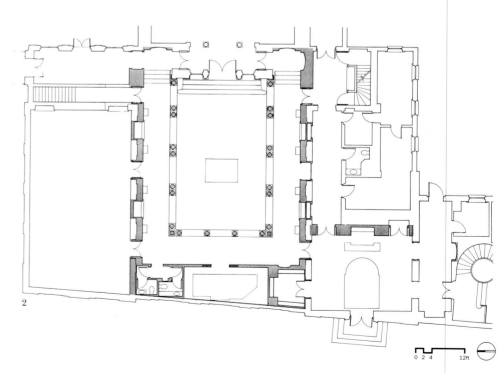

1   Site plan
2   Floor plan
3   The end of the gallery

176

Ionic columns reproduce those in the music room. McKim, Mead and White's Palladian window was retained. Unlike the music room, however, the new gallery is suffused with natural light from a glazed opening in the barrel-vaulted ceiling.

4

5

6

# Market Square

Design/Completion 1984/1990
701–801 Pennsylvania Avenue
Washington, DC
Trammell Crow Company
Washington, DC
1,117,000 square feet (including parking)
Post-tensioned concrete frame,
flat slabs and limestone columns
Indiana buff limestone; brick; architectural
precast concrete; custom aluminum
storefronts; aluminum windows and curtain wall
with painted metal spandrels

Market Square is a competition-winning
scheme for a pivotal site on Pennsylvania
Avenue. The shape, in plan, was dictated
by the Pennsylvania Avenue Development
Corporation. Bisecting Market Square's
twin, mirror-image, mixed-use buildings
is the only cross axis along the Avenue
which connects the White House and the
Capitol. This cross axis places Market
Square in the path joining the Portrait
Gallery, located two blocks to the north,
with the National Archives Building, which
faces the new complex across the Avenue.
The axis continues across the Mall
to terminate at the Hirshhorn Museum.
Market Square's curved buildings, cupping
the crescent-shaped Navy Memorial,
further mark the midpoint between the
capital city's executive and legislative
realms while straddling the line between
official Washington to the south and the
city's commercial downtown
to the north.

*Continued*

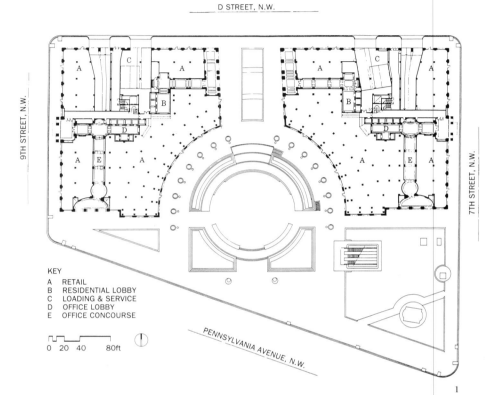

KEY
A RETAIL
B RESIDENTIAL LOBBY
C LOADING & SERVICE
D OFFICE LOBBY
E OFFICE CONCOURSE

0 20 40 80ft

1

2

1 Site plan
2 Market Square from the south-east
3 National Archives from between the two buildings
4 South elevation of east wing

3

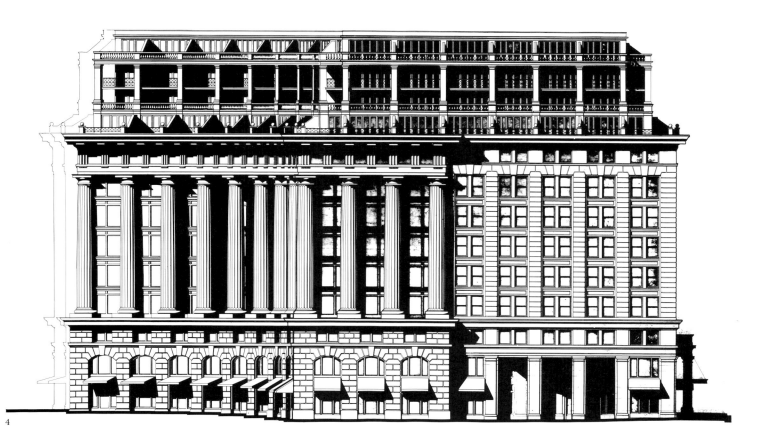

4

The complex contains 584,000 square feet of office space, 70,000 square feet of retail, and 250 penthouse apartments. It continues the neoclassical vocabulary of the Federal Triangle immediately to its southwest.

The office space is expressed in glass and aluminum curtain walls, while the residential units are housed in the buildings' top four stories, which step back twice to create terraces. At ground level the complex has retail space for office tenants on Seventh and Ninth streets, and for residents on Eighth street. Ground floor space on the memorial crescent is devoted to restaurants and the Navy Visitors' Center, while office entrances are on Pennsylvania Avenue.

Morris Architects was the associated architect for construction documents and site observation.

5

6

5 Market Square from the National Archives with the
 Navy Memorial in the foreground
6 The south-west corner showing residential units over the
 office and commercial space
7 Colonnade on the east block
8 The axis up Eighth street to the Old Patent Office Building

7

8

# One Franklin Square Building

Design/Completion 1985/1990
1301 K Street, NW
Washington, DC
Prentiss Properties Ltd.
Washington, DC
1,032,000 square feet (including parking)
Reinforced concrete frame with flat slabs
Spanish pink granite; architectural precast concrete;
custom aluminum storefronts; white Carrara and Fior di Pesco marble;
terra cotta; aluminum window frames with insulating clear glass;
terne-coated stainless steel and membrane roofs

The most striking aspect of One Franklin
Square is its twin towers, which identify
the building from afar and provide
the predominantly low-rise city with
a new landmark. The office tower was
aligned with Franklin Square which forms
the building's front yard across K Street,
one of Washington's major commercial
arteries. Specific design cues were derived
from Franklin Square's two venerable
next-door neighbors to the west.
The system of bays and towers was
suggested by the Beaux-Arts Hamilton
Hotel and serves to visually break down
the building's great length. The entrance
configuration reflects that of the 1926
Moorish-style Almas Temple, which
was moved slightly to accommodate
One Franklin Square.

The 210-foot-high towers were permitted
to exceed the city's 11-story height limit
because they are "unoccupied
embellishments".

*Continued*

1

184

2

The architects differentiated them from the body of the building by pulling them forward, and then broke down the building's length by defining a series of bays. They further mitigated its bulk by setbacks at the eighth and tenth floors, by striping, and by recessing windows to create a pattern of dark shadows. Dewberry and Davis/Habib was the associated architect for construction documents and site observation. Oehrlein and Associates was the historic preservation consultant.

3

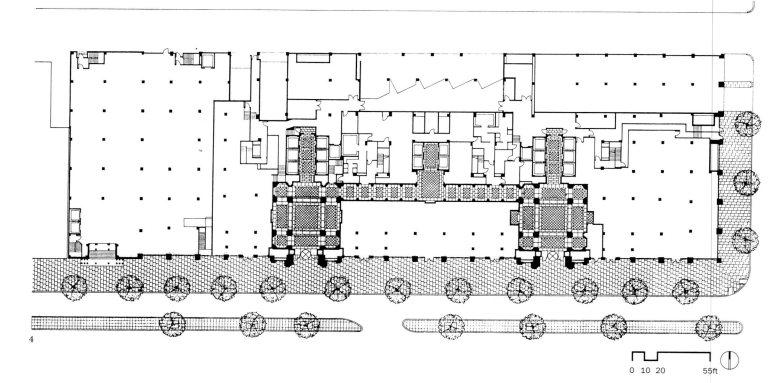

4

0 10 20        55ft

5

# Pennsylvania Plaza

Design/Completion 1987/1990
601 Pennsylvania Avenue, NW
Washington, DC
The Sigal/Zuckerman Company, Washington, DC
and The Lawrence Ruben Company, New York
445,000 square feet (excluding parking)
Reinforced concrete frame with flat slabs
Granite; Indiana limestone; brick; architectural precast concrete;
custom aluminum storefronts; aluminum window frames with
insulating clear glass; decorative metal rails; marble on interior

Pennsylvania Plaza comprises two
connected buildings with different uses
on a tight trapezoidal site. The office
block contains 300,000 square feet of
office space while the apartment
component contains 145,000 square feet
on 14 floors. The offices, each providing
16,000 square feet of leasable space, are
located on the western portion of the lot
to capture views of Pennsylvania Avenue,
while the complex's 150 apartments wrap
around the eastern corner to receive the
morning sun. The office building's precast
forms are reminiscent of 19th century cast-
iron Italianate buildings, while the
apartment building's red and buff brick
tower recalls similar, nearby corner
treatments.

The office building's poured-in-place
structure with precast panels leaves the
interior perimeter of floors relatively
unobstructed. Space is organized along
the usual Washington grid with columns
20 feet on-center. Ground floor retail
includes a sidewalk café. The office lobby
is clad in beige limestone and marble.

1

2

1    Apartment building looking west towards Federal Triangle
2    East elevation of apartment building
3    Precast office building wall

3

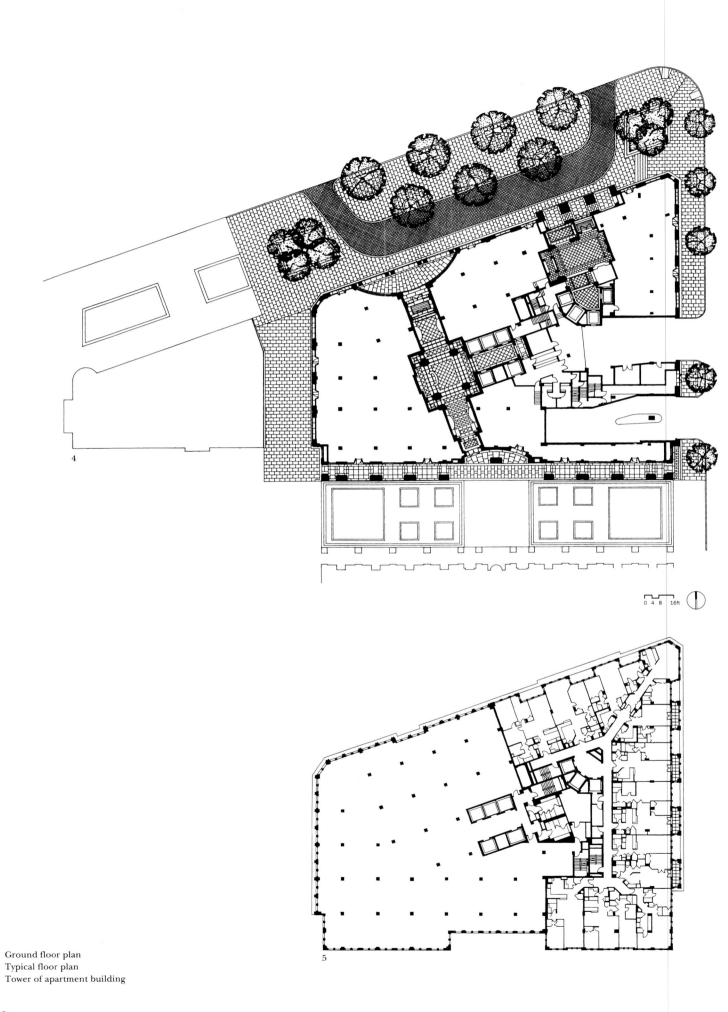

4   Ground floor plan
5   Typical floor plan
6   Tower of apartment building

6

## 800 North Capitol Street

Design/Completion 1989/1991
Washington, DC
800 North Capitol Limited Partnership, Washington, DC
390,000 square feet (including parking)
Reinforced concrete frame with flat slabs
Granite; brick on CMU back-up; architectural precast concrete; custom aluminum storefronts;
aluminum window frames with insulating clear glass

This office building provides 300,000 square feet of office and retail space and 90,000 square feet of below-grade parking a short distance from the Capitol. In its materials and motifs, it complements the Government Printing Office, a full-block, 19th century red brick structure just across the street, and the Gonzaga campus further to the north. Its cornice lines and fenestration continue a strong pattern established by the GPO and its rusticated base and deep Romanesque bays echo the Gonzaga detailing.

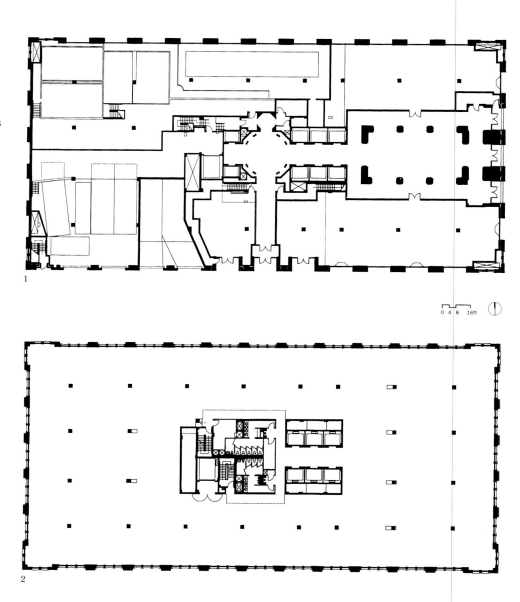

1

2

1 Ground floor plan
2 Typical floor plan
3 East facade

3

4  Looking south towards the Capitol
5  Detail of facade
6  At street level
7  Detail of stone and brick arches

4

5

6

7

# 1501 M Street, NW

Design/Completion 1988/1991
Washington, DC
Shannon & Luchs/Kossow Development Company
Washington, DC
265,000 square feet (including parking)
Reinforced concrete frame with flat slabs
Architectural precast concrete exterior; aluminum,
GFRC and glass window wall; lead-coated copper dome

This corner office building is deliberately reminiscent of the early 20th century cast iron buildings in the lower Manhattan area of New York City. The ranks of Doric columns are detached from the curtain wall facade behind them, creating a non-structural cage. Classical motifs are continued with the use of arched bays and deep cornices at the base. The tower ties down the corner. The building includes 187,000 square feet of office space, 78,000 square feet below grade, and a 7,000 square foot penthouse.

1

1   East facade
2   Detail looking up
3   Ground floor plan
4   Typical floor plan

2

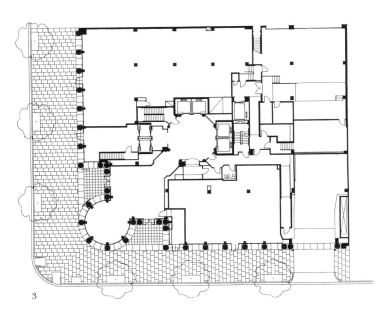

3

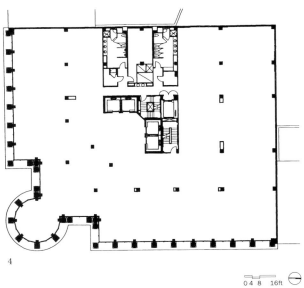

4

0 4 8  16ft

# John Carter Brown Library Addition and Renovation

Design/Completion 1987/1991
Brown University
Providence, Rhode Island
Brown University
15,000 square foot addition
6,000 square feet remodeled and renovated
Steel frame and metal deck with concrete slabs
Limestone; granite; custom aluminum grills; cast stone and carved ornament; built-up roof; VCT, wood and marble floors; custom oak millwork

The John Carter Brown Library is a rare book and manuscript library on the Brown University campus. Its collection of material on the early Americas is the best in this country, and one of the most important in the world. The original building was designed by Shepley, Rutan and Coolidge and built in 1904. The library was in great need of renovation and expansion.

The existing building is in a style generally called "neo-Grec". The new book vault addition continues the architectural character and material (limestone) of the original, although modifying its motifs considerably to accommodate a different function. The tall, vertical windows of the vault, for example, are traditionally associated with library stack areas. The addition is essentially a "tail" on what is otherwise a bilaterally symmetrical building.

With the exception of the reading room and front corner offices, the existing building has been extensively reworked to make it both more responsive to the change in needs and a more attractive and comfortable place to work.

1

1   Rear entrance
2   South elevation with addition
3   South elevation before addition

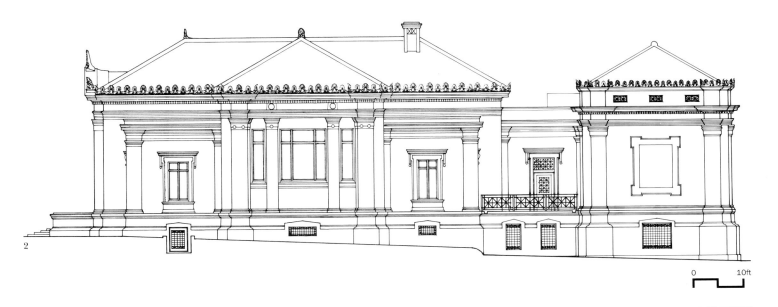

2

0　　　10ft

3

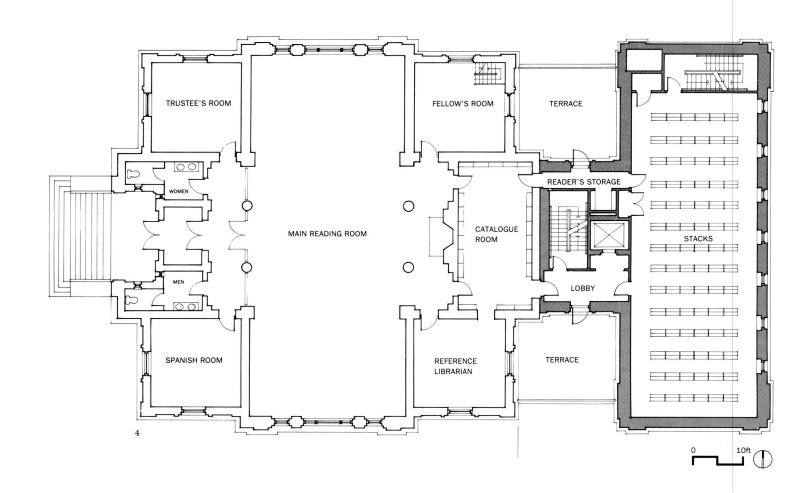

TRUSTEE'S ROOM

FELLOW'S ROOM

TERRACE

WOMEN

READER'S STORAGE

MEN

MAIN READING ROOM

CATALOGUE ROOM

STACKS

LOBBY

SPANISH ROOM

REFERENCE LIBRARIAN

TERRACE

4

0          10ft

4   First floor plan
5   East elevation of book vault

5

6

6  Existing front elevation
7  East elevation
8  South or street elevation with addition on right

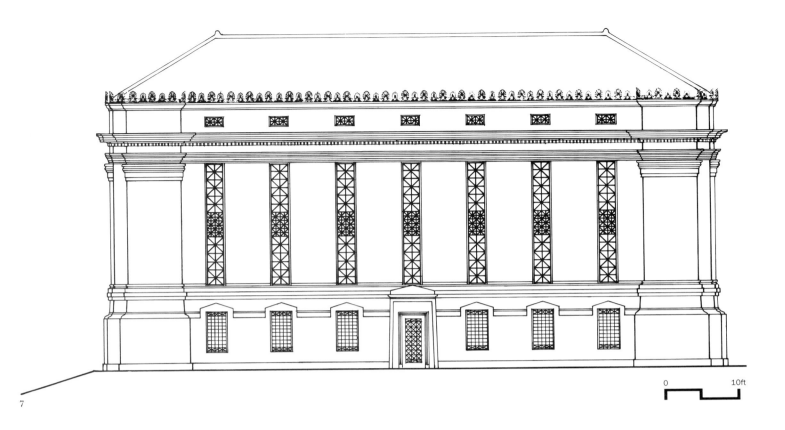

7

8

# Washington National Airport Parking Structure

Design/Completion 1988/1991
Washington National Airport
Washington, DC
Metropolitan Washington Airports Authority
787,000 square feet
Post-tensioned concrete frame
Architectural concrete; glass block; stainless steel

The South Parking Structure was the first major new building subsequent to the completion of the master plan for redevelopment of Washington's center-city airport. The structure maintains the visual line of the Metrorail bridge above and the roadway circulation at grade. This "non-building" holds 2,500 automobiles efficiently, at the same time screening them from the adjacent roadway. The parking structure steps back to resemble a terraced hillside which substantially lessens the impact of an otherwise large, objectionable, but necessary part of the airport environment.

At the middle of the garage is a curved glass block tower containing vertical circulation and directories. As the only vertical element in an otherwise horizontal structure, the circulation tower is the obvious point of reference. The form and material of both the concrete parking decks and the tower echo the design motifs of the original National Airport terminal.

Howard, Needles, Tammen and Bergendoff were associated architects.

1

1   Pedestrian lobby
2   The pedestrian entrance at night

2

# 1200 K Street, NW

Design/Completion 1988/1992
Washington, DC
Prudential Property Company, Inc.
Washington, DC
520,000 square feet (including parking)
Reinforced concrete frame with flat slabs
Brick on CMU and precast concrete; architectural precast concrete; granite; limestone; marble; custom aluminum storefronts; decorative metal railing; aluminum windows with insulating clear glass

1200 K Street is designed as a contextual response to related K Street buildings, most directly to the early and mid-20th century commercial buildings across the street and the neighboring 19th century Franklin School.

The decorative facades are intended to provide a maximum of fenestration, yet remain substantial and monumental. The design is articulated horizontally in a classical five-part scheme of bays and niches which are further divided vertically into base, middle and attic stories topped by a terraced roofscape.

Oehrlein and Associates was the historic preservation architect for the restoration of the Franklin School building.

1

2

1   From the north-west
2   Entrance
3   Facade at entrance

3

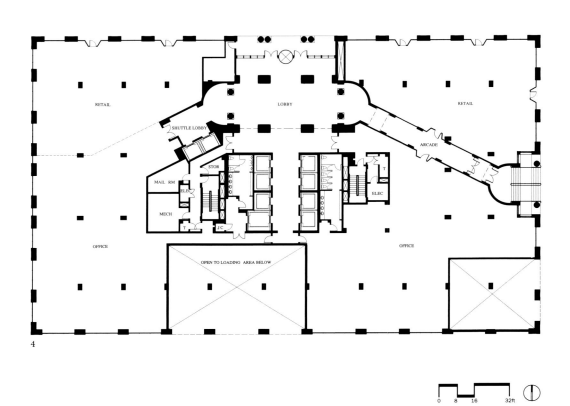

4

5

6

7

# New Exhibition Building, Winterthur Museum and Garden

Design/Completion 1988/1992
Henry Francis duPont Museum and Gardens
Wilmington, Delaware
Trustees of the Henry Francis DuPont Winterthur Museum
45,000 square foot addition
Additional remodeling and renovation in existing museum
Steel frame, steel deck and concrete slabs
Stucco on CMU; cast stone; custom wood trim and millwork;
custom aluminum curtain wall; flagstone, limestone and wood floors;
clay tile and membrane roofs; lead-coated copper gutters and downspouts

The New Exhibition Building is part of the program of the world's foremost museum of America decorative arts to open its collection to a wider audience. In the past, only guided tours of period rooms had been provided. With the New Exhibition Building, self-guided educational tours and exhibitions were made available.

The New Exhibition Building is connected to the entrance of the museum with a large, conservatory-like pavilion, echoing two conservatories elsewhere at Winterthur. This serves as a reception area and entrance to both elements of the museum. The rest of the addition of 45,000 square feet consists of stair and entry areas and two floors of open, "T"-shaped, flexible exhibition space. The addition runs across a shallow glen and bridges a small stream, terminating the long, downhill facade of the existing museum. The addition's scale, materials and form–stucco facing, hipped and tiled roofs, dormers and colonnaded porches– echo those of the original museum.

1

2

1   The original house as it is today
2   East entrance
3   From the south-west across Clenny Run
4   West elevation with existing building

3

4

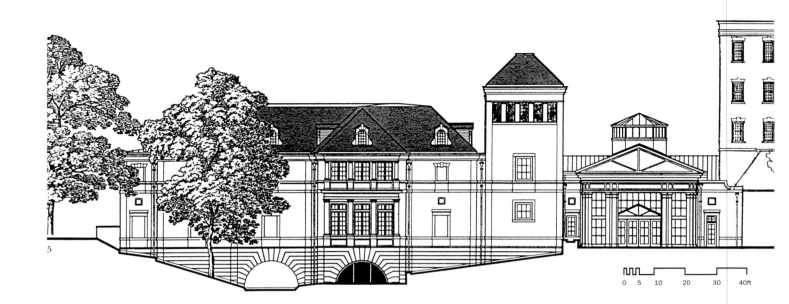

5

6

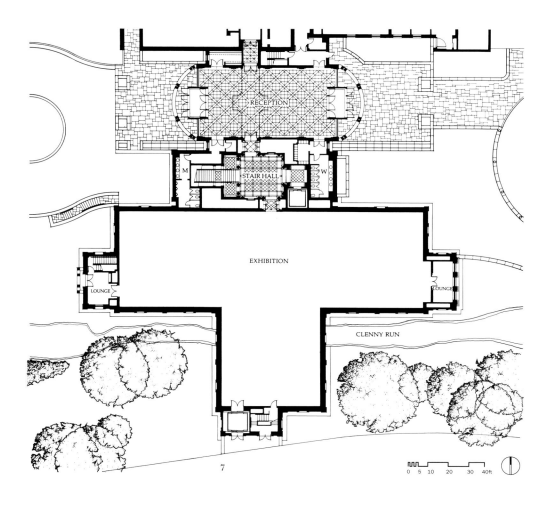

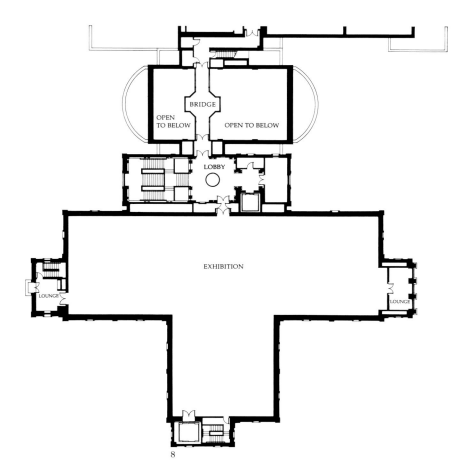

9 Reception hall linking the two buildings
10 Main staircase from lower landing
11 Second floor stair hall
12 Intermediate stair landing from below

9

10

11

12

New Exhibition Building, Winterthur Museum and Garden   215

13 Looking up to second level from stair hall
14 First floor stair hall and main staircase
15 Section
16 Second floor stair hall

13

14

15

0  5  10    20    30    40ft

# Georgetown University Law Center Residence Hall

Design/Completion 1988/1993
120 F Street, NW
Washington, DC
Georgetown University
213,000 square feet (including parking)
Post-tensioned reinforced concrete slabs
Brick; architectural precast concrete;
decorative metal rails; membrane roof

The residence hall is located to the south of the academic building and, with the law library to the north, forms a small, self-contained campus. The massing, scale, materials and architectural character of the residence hall are designed to complement these buildings.

The building is a 12-story slab with four additional levels below grade. One hundred fifty-four apartment units occupy ten of the floors.

The stepped massing of the building provides a variety of apartment unit sizes, conforms to zoning setback requirements, and creates a transition to the lower, four-story height of the other campus buildings. The entrance to the building faces the adjacent law center campus and is expressed by a cylindrical drum rising to the eleventh floor. This form contains residential lounges, and echoes the rotunda which forms the entrance to the law library. The building is constructed of limestone-colored precast concrete and brick, echoing the law library and academic building.

1

2

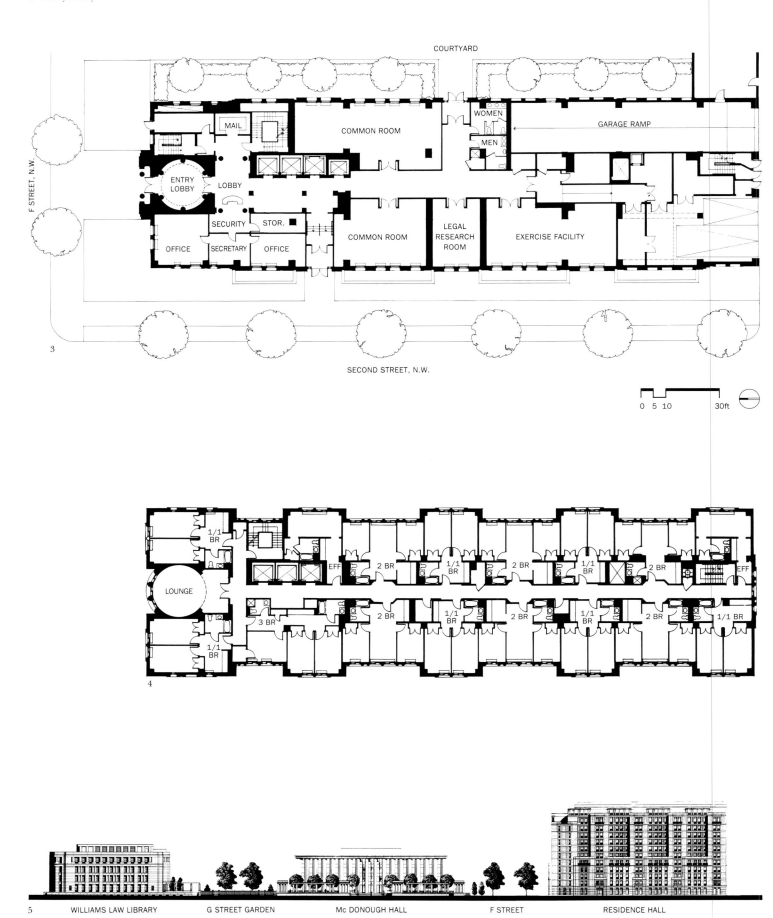

3

5   WILLIAMS LAW LIBRARY          G STREET GARDEN          Mc DONOUGH HALL          F STREET          RESIDENCE HALL

Georgetown University Law Center Residence Hall   221

7 From the north-east
8 West elevation
9 From across the sunken freeway

8

9

# Tulane University Law School

Design/Completion 1991/1994
New Orleans, Louisiana
Tulane University
150,000 square feet
Concrete frame with concrete beams
and pan system; pile foundations
Brick on CMU; custom aluminum curtain wall;
built-up roof; tile floor; custom wood trim

A new law school building containing library, classrooms, clinic, offices and computer lab is to be located on a mid-campus site that will form the fourth side of a quadrangle. The other buildings are two high-rise, 1960s gridded apartment slabs and the new, high-rise, post-modern business school. These buildings do not relate well to each other, and none offer a style to emulate.

The proposed building, while drawing certain design references—such as the ground floor arches and center bay—from the older, more handsome buildings elsewhere on the campus, attempts to emulate the character of a traditional law school building. This prototype is essentially neo-Romanesque or collegiate Gothic in character. The design places the library in a central, higher block with courtyards (a New Orleans tradition as well as a collegiate tradition) on either side. This allows the rest of the building to be three stories high, preserving the scale along Freret Street to the south and echoing the campus proper.

The Mathes Group is the local associated architect.

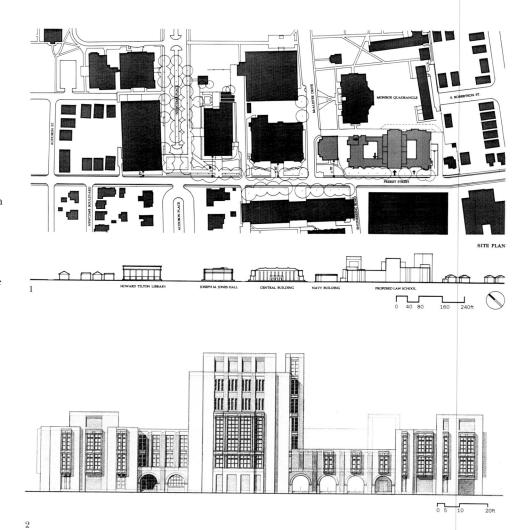

1

2

1   Site plan
2   North elevation
3   First floor plan
4   Third floor plan

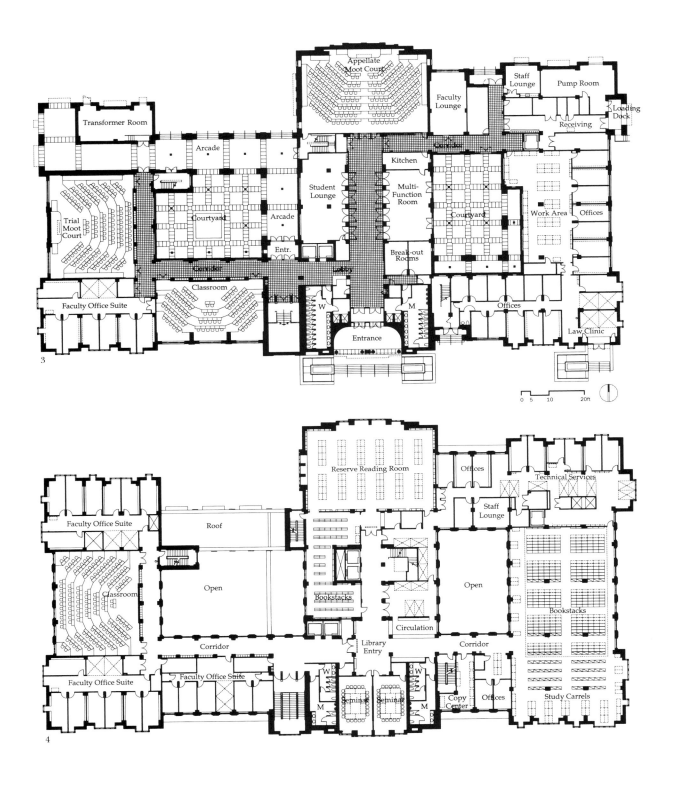

# University of Connecticut Law School Library

Design/Completion 1992/1995
Hartford, Connecticut
University of Connecticut
120,000 square feet
Steel frame
Random ashlar granite; architectural precast concrete;
slate roofs; custom oak millwork

This new law school library is to be located in the middle of a small, cohesive "collegiate Gothic" campus. The architects have been asked to design a building which will be compatible with the other campus buildings.

The library is arranged in a flexible, open plan with reader spaces and offices around the perimeter. Service facilities are located in areas towards the center.

While actually five stories high, the building is sited in a depression so that two floors will be below the entrance level. This allows the height above grade to match the existing buildings.

Quinn Associates, Inc. is the associated architect for construction documents and site observation.

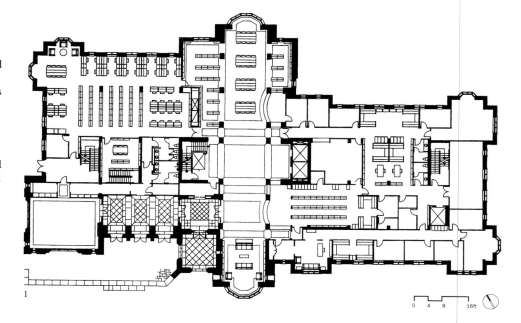

1   Floor plan at entrance level
2   South or entrance elevation

# Special Collections Library, University of Virginia

Design/Completion 1992/
University of Virginia, Charlottesville, Virginia
University of Virginia
78,000 square feet
Reinforced concrete frame, slabs and beams;
double slabs and walls
Double membrane roof; carpet and wood floors;
custom millwork

The library will house the rare books
and special collections of the university
with the goal of establishing an identity
separate from Alderman Library, the main
university library. Various solutions were
studied, including additions to Alderman
Library, renovation of existing buildings,
and new building sites. The proposed site
for the library is on the older part
of the university's campus, next to
Jefferson's Lawn and Alderman Library.
The proposal involves renovation
of an existing building adjacent to
Alderman to provide exhibition and
meeting space, and access to a new,
below-grade structure which will house
the main reading room and stack areas.

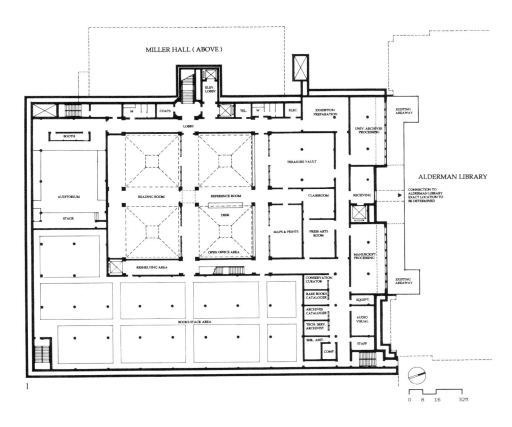

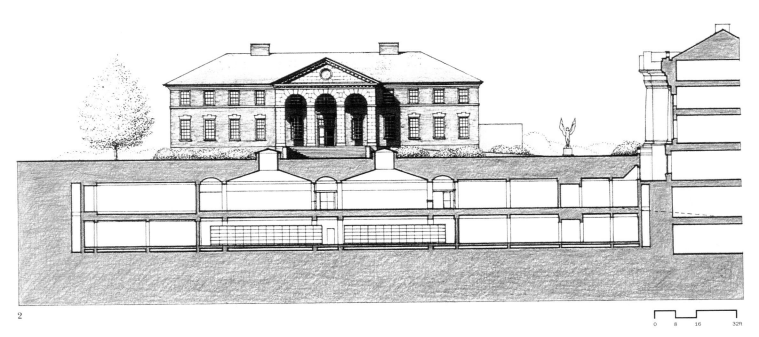

1   Floor plan
2   Sectional perspective looking north

# Preservation and Restoration of the Lincoln and Jefferson Memorials

Design/Completion 1988/2000
Washington, DC
US Department of the Interior/National Park Service/
Denver Service Center
Reinforced concrete frame and marble/limestone
columns (original buildings)
Granite; marble; limestone; brick; marble,
granite and cobblestone paving (original buildings)

This project involves creating
and implementing a preservation strategy
for the memorials following extensive
surveying, data collection, monitoring
and analysis of existing conditions.
The project was undertaken in a series
of carefully designed subprojects,
each of which had to be extensively
co-ordinated with the National Park
Service.

The architects were responsible
for identifying the preservation issues
and formulating an overall master plan
for preservation and restoration.
Construction documentation for various
aspects of the plan is currently underway.

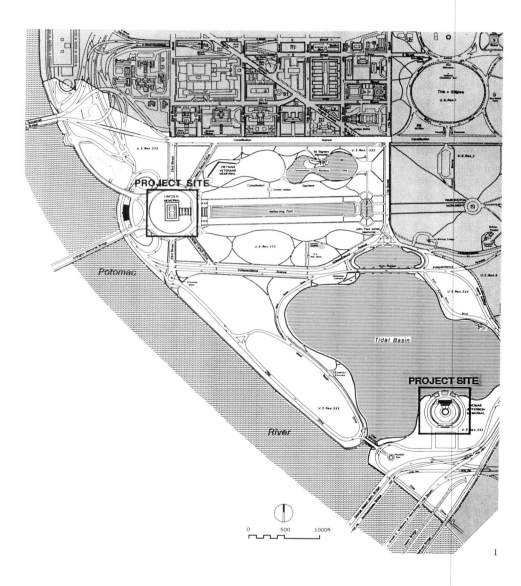

1

1   Site plan
2   The Lincoln Memorial
3   The Jefferson Memorial

2

3

# Firm Profile

# Background/Biography

**(L–R)**
**George E. Hartman Jr**
**and Warren J. Cox**

Hartman-Cox Architects was founded by George E. Hartman Jr and Warren J. Cox in 1965. Although the majority of their earlier projects were residential and relatively small, the firm soon obtained two larger and very visible non-residential commissions which produced immediate national recognition: the buildings at Mount Vernon College and the Euram Office Building on Dupont Circle in downtown Washington. More large commissions followed and, within the first few years of practice, the firm received two American Institute of Architects National Honor Awards and the first International Louis Sullivan Prize for architecture in masonry.

Over the past two and a half decades the firm has grown slowly to a size averaging 25 architects, and major institutions and developers have become clients. In addition to their corporate, academic, library and museum buildings, the firm completed a series of major commercial office buildings during the 1980s, all but one in Washington and five on or adjacent to Pennsylvania Avenue. Another important area of practice which developed at the same time was the restoration of or addition to prominent historic structures, since many of the firm's projects coincidentally involved this type of work as an adjunct to new buildings. Ultimately, it became a specialty.

With the recession of the early 1990s effectively eliminating the commercial market for the foreseeable future, the firm has been fortunate to expand its institutional and museum work. There are currently a significant number of academic, library, law school and museum commissions in progress throughout the country.

George Hartman received his BA from Princeton University in 1957, followed by his Master of Fine Arts in Architecture in 1960. He was then architect to Princeton's Archeological Excavation in Italy for a year, followed by four years as a designer at the Washington firm of Keyes, Lethbridge and Condon. He has taught at the University of Maryland and Catholic University in Washington, DC, and is a Fellow of the American Institute of Architects and the American Academy in Rome. He has served on the District of Columbia Joint Committee on Landmarks and is currently a member of the Commission of Fine Arts and the Architectural Review Panel of the Foreign Buildings Office of the Department of State. He has also served on numerous architectural design awards juries and has lectured throughout the country.

Warren Cox received his BA, *magna cum laude*, from Yale University in 1957, following with his Master in Architecture in 1961, again at Yale. He was editor of *Perspecta* magazine and received the Henry Adams Prize. While at Yale, Cox spent two summers working for the BBPR firm in Milan, Italy. After a year as Technology Editor of *Architectural Forum* magazine, he also became a designer at Keyes, Lethbridge and Condon until 1965. Warren Cox has taught at Yale University, Catholic University and the University of Virginia and is a Fellow of the American Institute of Architects. He has served on the Georgetown Board of the Commission of Fine Arts and the boards of the D.C. Preservation League and the Center for Palladian Studies in America. He, too, has served on a multitude of architectural design awards juries and lectured extensively throughout the country.

While George Hartman and Warren Cox have traditionally shared design and management responsibilities equally, in recent years the senior staff have come to take increasing responsibility for the practice. The firm has one junior partner, Mario H. Boiardi (BA, Princeton University, 1970; Master of Fine Arts in Architecture, Princeton University, 1972), and two associates, T. Lee Becker (Bachelor of Architecture, University of Maryland, 1974) and D. Graham Davidson (Bachelor of Architecture, University of Maryland, 1974), each of whom has been with the firm for over a dozen years. They have been involved in the design and management of virtually every major project in that period.

In 1988 Hartman-Cox Architects received the American Institute of Architects Architectural Firm Award, the highest award for architectural design a firm can receive from the Institute. Over the years, the firm has received over ninety other regional and national design awards including six AIA National Honor Awards and some sixteen historic preservation awards.

# Associates & Collaborators

## Associated Architects

Ballard, McKim & Sawyer, PC
Wilmington, North Carolina

Bassetti Norton Metler Rekevics, PC
Seattle, Washington

CHK Architects and Planners, Inc.
Silver Spring, Maryland

Chumney/Urrutia
San Antonio, Texas

Arthur Q. Davis & John C. Williams, PC
New Orleans, Louisiana

Dewberry & Davis
Fairfax, Virginia

Howard Needles Tammen & Bergendoff
Alexandria, Virginia

The Mathes Group
New Orleans, Louisiana

Morris Architects
Houston, Texas

Navy Marshall & Gordon, PC
Washington, DC

John Milner Associates
Philadelphia, Pennsylvania

Oehrlein Associates
Washington, DC

Quinn Associates, Inc.
New Britain, Connecticut

Shriver and Holland Associates
Norfolk, Virginia

Smith Segreti Tepper Architects &
Planners, PC
Washington, DC

## Consultants

AAAS Environmental, Inc.
Environmental Consultants
Bethesda, Maryland

Henry Adams, Inc.
Mechanical/Electrical/Plumbing
Engineers
Baltimore, Maryland

Air Survey Corporation
Aerial Photography Services
Sterling, Virginia

Arena & Company, Inc.
Construction/Design Management
Consultants
Wallingford, Pennsylvania

Peter Barna
Lighting Consultant
Washington, DC

Barton-Aschman Associates, Inc.
Parking Facilities Consultants
Evanston, Illinois

Bolt Beranek and Newman Inc.
Acoustical Engineers
Cambridge, Massachusetts

Brown & Associates
Security Consultants
Williamsburg, Virginia

Browne, Eichman, Dalgliesh, Gilpin &
Paxton, PC
Preservation Consultants
Charlottesville, Virginia

CBM Engineers, Inc.
Structural Engineers
Houston, Texas

CHK Architects and Planners, Inc.
Planning Consultants
Silver Spring, Maryland

Irwin G. Cantor
Consulting Structural Engineers
New York, New York

Cini-Little International, Inc.
Foodservice/Lodging Consultants
Potomac, Maryland

Clifton, Theobald Associates, Ltd.
Consulting Structural Engineers
Washington, DC

Lester Collins
Landscape Architect
Key West, Florida

Donald V. Colvin
Hardware Consultant
Washington, North Carolina

Cosentini Associates
Consulting Mechanical/Electrical/
Plumbing Engineers
New York, New York

F.M. Costantino, Inc.
Illustrator of Architecture/Perspectivist
Winthrop, Massachusetts

Coventry Lighting Associates
Lighting Consultants
Washington, DC

James Madison Cutts
Consulting Structural Engineers
Washington, DC

Dennett, Muessig, Ryan & Associates, Ltd.
Photogrammetry Services
Iowa City, Iowa

Anthony Di Camillo
General Technical Consultant
College Park, Maryland

Eastern Irrigation Consultants
Incorporated
Irrigation Consultants
Beltsville, Maryland

Engineering and Technical
Consultants, Inc.
Roof Consultants
Sterling, Virginia

Claude R. Engle
Lighting Consultants
Washington, DC

Figueroa & Doss
Professional Rendering Services
New York, New York

Flack + Kurtz
Consulting Mechanical/Electrical/
Plumbing Engineers
New York, New York

Foster-Crowder Design
Interior Design Consultants
Washington, DC

Froehling & Robertson, Inc.
Geotechnical/Environmental/Materials
Engineers
Richmond, Virginia

Gage-Babcock & Associates, Inc.
Code Consultants
Wheaton, Illinois

Girard Engineering, Ltd.
Mechanical/Electrical/Plumbing
Engineers
McLean, Virginia

Glassman & Associates, PC
Consulting Mechanical/Electrical/
Plumbing Engineers
Vienna, Virginia

Grenald Associates, Ltd.
Architectural Lighting Consultants
Narberth, Pennsylvania

Delon Hampton
Civil Engineers
Washington, DC

Hanscomb Associates, Inc.
Construction Cost Consultants
Chicago, Illinois

Ann Hartman
Interior Design Consultant
Chevy Chase, Maryland

Heitmann & Associates Inc.
Professional Cladding Consultants
St Louis, Missouri

Hoffmann Architects
Roof Consultants
North Haven, Connecticut

International Architectural
Rendering Ltd.
Professional Rendering Services
Nassau, Bahamas

IMC Consulting Engineers, Inc.
Mechanical/Electrical/Plumbing
Engineers
Metaire, Louisiana

Rolf Jensen & Associates, Inc.
Fire Protection Engineers/Building
Code Consultants
Deerfield, Illinois

Johns & Hausmann Design Company
Architectural Woodwork
San Antonio, Texas

KCE Structural Engineers, PC
Structural Engineers
Washington, DC

James E. Keeter
Landscape Architect
San Antonio, Texas

Kulkarni Consultants, PC
Civil/Structural Engineers
Metaire, Louisiana

LDL Associates
Construction Specifications/Methods/
Materials Consultants
Jenkintown, Pennsylvania

Lee-Thorp, Inc.
Mechanical/Electrical Engineers
McLean, Virginia

Lerch, Bates & Associates Inc.
Transportation Consultants
Littleton, Colorado

Bernard F. Locraft
Civil Engineers
Washington, DC

Joseph R. Loring & Associates, Inc.
Consulting Engineers
New York, New York

Nash M. Love and Associates, Inc.
Consulting Mechanical/Electrical/

Plumbing Engineers/Facility Planners
Springfield, Virginia

Michael Marshall
Professional Rendering Services
Washington, DC

Donald H. Messersmith
Entomology/Ornithology Consultant
College Park, Maryland

Miller Henning Associates, Inc.
Acoustics/Vibration/Audiovisual Design
Consultants
Washington, DC

Mitchell & Company Graphic Design, Inc.
Graphic Design Consultants and Services
Washington, DC

Walter Moleski/Environmental Research
Group
Programming Consultants
Philadelphia, Pennsylvania

Walter P. Moore and Associates, Inc.
Consulting Engineers/Planners
San Antonio, Texas

Roger Morgan Studio, Inc.
Theatre Design Consultants
New York, New York

Robert L. Morris, Inc.
Traffic/Transportation Consultants
Bethesda, Maryland

Mueller Associates II, Inc.
Consulting Mechanical/Electrical/
Plumbing Engineers
Baltimore, Maryland

National Fire Safety Engineering, Inc.
Fire Protection Consultants
Beltsville, Maryland

Newmont Elevator Analysts Inc.
Elevator/Escalator/People Mover
Engineering Consultants
St James, New York

Oehrlein & Associates
Preservation Consultants
Washington, DC

Paul Stevenson Oles, FAIA
Perspectivist
Newton, Massachusetts

Meade Palmer
Landscape Architect
Warrenton, Virginia

Polysonics
Acoustical Consultants
Washington, DC

RTKL, Inc.
Preservation Consultants
Baltimore, Maryland

Peter G. Rolland
Site Planners/Landscape Architects
Rye, New York

SME Consulting Engineers Inc.
Mechanical/Electrical Engineers
Rockville, Maryland

Scarf Godfrey Inc.
Construction Cost Consultants
Washington, DC

Schirmer Engineering Corporation
Fire Protection/Safety Engineers/
Building Code Consultants
Deerfield, Illinois

Richard Shank Associates, PC
Construction Consultants
Charlottesville, Virginia

Shefferman & Bigelson Company
Consulting Mechanical/Electrical/
Plumbing Engineers
Silver Spring, Maryland

Silber & Associates Consulting
Engineers, Inc.
Mechanical/Electrical/Plumbing
Engineers
San Antonio, Texas

W.E. Simpson Inc.
Civil/Structural Engineers
San Antonio, Texas

Smith & Faass
Consulting Mechanical/Electrical/
Plumbing Engineers
Germantown, Maryland

William L. Spack
Perspectivist
Arlington, Virginia

Everett G. Spurling, Jr.
Construction Specifications Consultant
Bethesda, Maryland

Raiford Stripling
Preservation Consultant
Austin, Texas

A. Morton Thomas and Associates, Inc.
Engineers/Surveyors/Planners/
Landscape Architects
Rockville, Maryland

James Urban
Landscape Architect
Annapolis, Maryland

# Associates & Collaborators

Urban Forest Management, Inc.
Tree Care Consultants and Services
Fairfax, Virginia

John A. Van Deusen & Associates Inc.
Building Transportation Systems
Consultants
Livingston, New Jersey

Vandemark & Lynch, Inc.
Engineers/Planners/Surveyors
Wilmington, Delaware

Michael Vergason
Landscape Architect
Arlington, Virginia

R. Kenneth Weeks
Sewage/Water Supply Consultants
Norfolk, Virginia

Stewart White Studios
Professional Rendering Services
Washington, DC

Curt Willard
Professional Rendering Services
Washington, DC

John Zeissel/Building Diagnostics, Inc.
Programming Consultant
Boston, Massachusetts

## Hartman-Cox Principals

George E. Hartman Jr
Warren J. Cox

## Partners

Mario H. Boiardi*

## Associates

T. Lee Becker*
D. Graham Davidson*

## Employees, 1965–1993

Stephen Banigan
Nancy Barba
Anthony Barnes
Eugene Bishop
Joseph Boggs
Calvert Bowie
Keith Brown
David Buergler
Susan Buttolph

John Carhart
Laurel Chamberlain
Matthew Cloud
Anthony Consoli
Susan Cox (Slade)
William Curtis

John Dale*
Frederica Davidson
Carmel Deckelman
Luciana Divine
David Drews
Elizabeth Driskill
Kenneth Drucker
Robert Dudka
David Duncan
David Duquette
Alan Dynerman

Thomas Eichbaum

Jonathan Fishman
Thomas Fowler

Karen Furnari

William Gaffney
Edward Gavagan
Ralph Giammatteo
Christopher Glass
William Grater
Elizabeth Greenberg
Mary Griffin (Turnbull)
Peter Grina*

Scott Hayward
Sarah Hartman
Johannes Haug
Amalie Hermes
Jessica Holmes
Marian Holmes*
Outerbridge Horsey
Richard Houghton

Karen Ianuzi

Gary Jacquemain
Anne Jaffe
Michael Johnson
Dianne Jonassen
David Jones

Ho Kang
Timothy Kearney
Andrea Kemler
William Kline
Kathleen Knepp
Son Kong

Mary Katherine Lanzillotta
Bryan Lavie*
Lisa Lee
Erica Ling
William Linton
Thomas Luebke

Michael Marshall
Guyman Martin
Gail McClure
John McConnell
Roxanne Mendoza

Phoebe Millon
Charles Moore
Steven Morken
Deana Morrison
Stephen Muse

John Nammack
William Neudorfer*

Judah Organic
Michael Orscheln

Keith Peoples
Matthew Poe
Bora Popovic
David Pugh

Annette Raynor
Phillip Renfrow
Douglas Rixey
Brian Robertson
David Robins
John Ross
Stacy Rudnick

Daniel St. Clair
Roland Schaaf
Constantine Seremetis
Vinay Shroff
Robert Shutler*
Lina Sibert
Susan Smyth
Christopher Snowber
Michael Stanton
David Sternberg
Andrew Stevenson*
James Stokoe
Claire Strasser

Frederick Taylor
Kristin Terry
Susan Terry
Cathleen Thurber

Joye Vailes
Stephen Vanze*
Deborah Vischak

Alexandros Washburn
Julian Weiss
Ruth Wells
Rosalie Wilkinson
John Williams
Richard Williams
Stephanie Wilson
Gay Wimer
Marc Wouters
Christopher Wynn

Elizabeth Zadravec
Alexander Zaras*

* Indicates employees who have been or were
  with the firm eight years or longer.

# Chronological List of Buildings & Projects

*Indicates work featured in this book
(see Selected and Current Works).

**Victorian Duplex Renovation**
1965
Washington, DC
Mr and Mrs George E. Hartman

**Residential Additions**
1965–1968
Washington, DC
Hon. James Symington

**Ball Room**
1966–1968
Washington, DC
Embassy of Saudi Arabia

**Office, 1310 19th Street, NW**
1966–1968
Washington, DC
Hon. James Symington

**Victorian Townhouse Office Conversion**
1966–1969
Washington, DC
Washington Metropolitan Chapter/
American Institute of Architects

**Victorian Renovation and Addition**
1966–1968
Washington, DC
Mr and Mrs Ronald Scheman

**Residential Addition**
1966–1969
Bethesda, Maryland
Mr and Mrs Harold Tager

**Long Range Development Plan**
1966
Washington, DC
Mount Vernon College

**\*College Chapel**
1967–1970
Washington, DC
Mount Vernon College

**Fairfax Village Recreational Center**
1967–1969
Washington, DC
National Park Service

**\*Private Residence**
1967–1969
Chevy Chase, Maryland
Phillips/Brewer families

**Victorian House Renovation**
1967–1969
Washington, DC
Mr and Mrs Jeremy Blanchet

**Victorian Rooming House Renovation**
1967
Washington, DC
Estate of O.S. Cox

**Residential Addition**
1967–1969
Washington, DC
Judge and Mrs Harold Leventhal

**\*Euram Building**
1968–1971
Washington, DC
Euram Corporation

**\*Tennis Building**
1968–1970
Washington, DC
St Alban's School

**Colonial Townhouses,
Renovation and Addition**
1968–1970
Washington, DC
Mr and Mrs William Crocker

**Residential Addition**
1968–1971
Washington, DC
Mr and Mrs William Watts

**\*College Dormitory**
1969–1972
Washington, DC
Mount Vernon College

**Gate House**
1969–1972
Washington, DC
Mount Vernon College

**\*Stable**
1969–1972
Rock Creek Park, Washington, DC
National Park Service

**Victorian Townhouse Office Conversion**
1969
Washington, DC
National Council of Architectural
Registration Boards
*Not constructed*

**Federal Townhouse Office Conversion**
1969
Washington, DC
Hartman-Cox Architects

**Victorian Townhouse Renovation**
1970
Washington, DC
Mr and Mrs Warren J. Cox

**Victorian House Renovation
and Addition**
1970–1972
Washington, DC
Mr and Mrs David Kenney

**\*Barn and House,
Saltonstall Farm**
1970–1973
Rappahannock County, Virginia
Mrs Patricia Saltonstall

**Tennis Stadium**
1971
Washington, DC
Washington Area Tennis
Patrons Foundation
*Not constructed*

**Deck and Remodeling**
1971
Washington, DC
Mr and Mrs O. Mallory Walker

**\*Private Residence**
1972–1975
Potomac, Maryland

**Residence Rooms Renovation**
1972
Washington, DC
Cosmos Club

**Study, Student Lounge**
1972
Washington, DC
St Alban's School

**Dodge Center**
1973–1976
Washington, DC
Maloney Concrete Company

**Pyramid Gallery**
1973
Washington, DC
Pyramid Gallery

**Study, Visitor Center Addition,
Washington Monument**
1973
Washington, DC
National Park Service

**Study, Recreation Centers**
1973
Department of the Army

**Study, Carousel Enclosure**
1973
Washington, DC
Smithsonian Institution

**\*National Permanent Building**
1974–1977
Washington, DC
Lenkin Company

**Law Enforcement Center**
1974–1977
Wilmington, North Carolina
New Hanover County Commissioners

**\*Bookstore in the National Visitors'
Center, Union Station**
1974–1976
Washington, DC
National Park Service

**Office Addition**
1974–1977
Silver Spring, Maryland
Maryland National Capitol
Park & Planning Commission

**Private Residence**
1974
St Mary's County, Maryland

**Pool Addition**
1974–1976
Washington, DC
Mr and Mrs Philip B. Brown

**Preservation Plan for Urban Core**
1974
Wilmington, North Carolina
New Hanover County Commissioners

**\*National Humanities Center**
1976–1978
Research Triangle Park,
Raleigh, North Carolina
Triangle University Center for
Advanced Studies Inc.

**\*Library Additions and Renovation,
Folger Shakespeare Library**
1976–1982
Washington, DC
Trustees of Amherst College

**Office Interiors**
1976
Washington, DC
Koteen & Burt

**Office Interiors**
1976
Washington, DC
Financial General Bankshares Inc.

**Study, Resort Hotel Complex**
1976
Williamsburg, VA
Turner Construction Company

**Study, Space Planning and Interiors,
Headquarters Building**
1977
Washington, DC
American Institute of Architects

**\*US Embassy Office Building**
1978–1983
Kuala Lumpur, Malaysia
US Department of State

**\*Church**
1978–1980
McLean, Virginia
Immanuel Presbyterian Church

**Office Building**
1978
Washington, DC
American Psychiatric Association
*Not constructed*

**Fellows' Building Renovation, Dumbarton Oaks**
1978–1980
Washington, DC
Trustees of Harvard University

**\*Residential Additions**
1978–1981 & 1989
Washington, DC

**Residential Addition**
1978
Washington, DC
Mr and Mrs Steven Guttman

**Residential Addition**
1978–1980
Chevy Chase, Maryland
Mr and Mrs Henry G. Zapruder

**Study, Freer Gallery Courtyard Enclosure**
1979
Washington, DC
Smithsonian Institution

**Master Plan**
1979
Tarrytown, New York
International Business Machines

**"Kennersley", Restoration and Stabilization**
1979
Queen Anne's County, Maryland
Mr and Mrs Warren J. Cox

**\*1001 Pennsylvania Avenue**
1979–1986
Washington, DC
Cadillac Fairview Urban
Development Inc.

**Residential Addition**
1979
Chevy Chase, Maryland

**\*4250 Connecticut Avenue, NW**
1980–1983
Washington, DC
Prudential Insurance Company
of America

**\*HEB Headquarters Complex**
1981–1985
San Antonio, Texas
H.E. Butt Grocery Company

**\*Church and School**
1981–1986
Washington, DC
St Patrick's Church and Day School

**\*Private Residence**
1981–1983
McLean, Virginia
Mr and Mrs P. Wesley Foster

**Study, Music Conservatory**
1981
Washington, DC
Kennedy Center for the
Performing Arts

**Study, Addition and Renovation, Darden School of Business**
1981
Charlottesville, Virginia
University of Virginia

**\*Apex Building (exterior)**
1982–1984
Washington, DC
Historic Central Bank
Redevelopment Group

**\*Museum Additions and Renovation**
1982–1989
Norfolk, Virginia
Chrysler Museum

**Bookstore and Shop, National Museum of American History**
1982
Washington, DC
Smithsonian Institution

**\*Gallery Row**
1983–1986
Washington, DC
Carly Capital Group

**\*Sumner School Complex**
1983–1986
Washington, DC
17 M Associates

**\*Private Residence**
1983–1986
Washington, DC

**\*Market Square**
1984–1990
Washington, DC
Trammell Crow Company

**\*Law Library**
1984–1989
Washington, DC
Georgetown University Law Center

**\*Monroe Hall Addition**
1984–1987
Charlottesville, Virginia
McIntire School of Commerce,
University of Virginia

**Office Interiors**
1984
Washington, DC
Caplin & Drysdale

**\*One Franklin Square**
1985–1990
Washington, DC
Prentiss Properties Ltd

**\*Commerce Place**
1985
Baltimore, Maryland
Harlan Company
*Not constructed*

**\*Museum Additions and Renovation,
Dumbarton Oaks**
1985–1990
Washington, DC
Trustees of Harvard University

**\*Office Building Addition
and Master Plan**
1985–1987
Washington, DC
Corcoran Gallery of Art
*Not constructed*

**Private Residence**
1985–1989
Washington, DC

**Sutter's Court**
1986–1988
Washington, DC
L.M. & W. Properties Company
*Not constructed*

**Office Interiors**
1986
Washington, DC
Fried, Frank, Harris, Shriver
& Jacobson

**\*Pennsylvania Plaza**
1987–1990
Washington, DC
Sigal/Zuckerman Company and
Lawrence Reuben Company

**\*Library Addition and Renovation,
John Carter Brown Rare Book Library**
1987–1991
Providence, Rhode Island
Brown University

**Addition and Renovation**
1987–1991
Washington, DC
Georgetown University Law Center

**Bowen Building**
1987–1989
Washington, DC
International Masonry Institute
*Not constructed*

**Residential Addition and Renovation**
1987–1989
Washington, DC
Mr and Mrs Ralph Dweck

**Residential Addition**
1987–1988
Washington, DC
Mr and Mrs Roger Sant

**Master Plan for National Airport**
1987–1989
Washington, DC
Metropolitan Washington
Airports Authority

**\*1200 K Street, NW**
1988–1992
Washington, DC
Prudential Property Company Inc.

**\*1501 M Street, NW**
1988–1991
Washington, DC
Shannon & Luchs/Kossow
Development Company

**\*Residence Hall**
1988–1993
Washington, DC
Georgetown University Law Center

**Museum Addition and Renovation**
1988–1993
Wilmington, Delaware
Henry Francis duPont Winterthur
Museum and Gardens

**\*South Parking Structure**
1988–1991
Washington National Airport
Metropolitan Washington
Airports Authority

**Carroll Court**
1988–1990
Washington, DC
Kaempfer Company
*Not constructed*

**\*Preservation, Lincoln and
Jefferson Memorials**
1988–2000
Washington, DC
National Park Service

**\*800 North Capitol Street, NW**
1989–1991
Washington, DC
800 North Capitol
Limited Partnership

**26th and Pennsylvania
Avenue Apartments**
1989–1991
Washington, DC
Bennett & Owens
*Not constructed*

**Bookstore and Shop,
Folger Shakespeare Library**
1989–1990
Washington, DC
Trustees of Amherst College

**Master Planning Study,
Headquarters Building**
1990
Washington, DC
National Academy of Sciences

**\*Law School and Library**
1991–1994
New Orleans, Louisiana
Tulane University

**Newcomb Art Building,
Addition and Renovation**
1991–1995
New Orleans, Louisiana
Tulane University

**Private Residence**
1991–1992
Healdsburg, California
Mr and Mrs Thomas C. Reed

**Master Planning and
Technical Feasibility Study,
General Post Office Building**
1991
Washington, DC
Smithsonian Institution

**Feasibility Study, Kent Hall**
1991–1992
St Mary's City, Maryland
St Mary's College

**Kelvin Smith Library**
1992–1996
Cleveland, Ohio
Case Western Reserve University

**\*Law Library**
1992–1995
Hartford, Connecticut
University of Connecticut

**Law School and Library**
1992–1995
St Louis, Missouri
Washington University

**\*Special Collections Building,
Alderman Library**
1992–Indefinite
Charlottesville, Virginia
University of Virginia

**Residential Addition**
1992–1993
Bethesda, Maryland
Dr and Mrs Stuart F. Seides

**Master Plan for Medical Center**
1992–1993
Philadelphia, Pennsylvania
University of Pennsylvania

**Master Planning Study**
1992–1993
Hartford, Connecticut
Trinity College

**Physics Hall Addition**
1993–1996
Seattle, Washington
University of Washington

**Mather Hall**
1993–1994
Hartford, Connecticut
Trinity College

**Private Residence**
1993–1995
Bethesda, Maryland
Mr and Mrs Robert K. Tanenbaum

# Awards & Exhibitions

## Awards

**National Honor Award**
American Institute of Architects
Chrysler Museum
Norfolk, Virginia
1994

**Award for Excellence for Extraordinary Achievement in Architecture**
Washington Metropolitan Chapter/
American Institute of Architects
1200 K Street, Washington, DC
1993

**Award for Excellence for Extraordinary Achievement in Architecture**
Washington Metropolitan Chapter/
American Institute of Architects
800 North Capitol Street,
Washington, DC
1993

**Award for Excellence for Extraordinary Achievement in Historic Resources**
Washington Metropolitan Chapter/
American Institute of Architects
John Carter Brown Library,
Providence, Rhode Island
1993

**Brick in Architecture Award**
American Institute of Architects
and Brick Institute of America
800 North Capitol Street,
Washington, DC
1993

**Special Recognition**
Precast/Prestressed Concrete Institute
1501 M Street, Washington, DC
1993

**First Award**
Masonry Institute
South Parking Structure,
Washington National Airport
1992

**Award for Design Excellence**
Architectural Precast Association
800 North Capitol Street,
Washington, DC
1992

**Certificate of Merit**
Associated Builders and Contractors/
Washington Metropolitan and
Virginia Chapters
800 North Capitol Street,
Washington, DC
1992

**Honorable Mention**
Institutional and Municipal
Parking Congress
South Parking Structure,
Washington National Airport
1992

**Award for Excellence for Extraordinary Achievement in Historic Preservation/ Renovation**
Washington Metropolitan Chapter/
American Institute of Architects
Dumbarton Oaks Museum,
Washington, DC
1991

**Award for Excellence for Extraordinary Achievement in Architecture**
Washington Metropolitan Chapter/
American Institute of Architects
Georgetown University Law Center
Library, Washington, DC
1991

**Merit Award for Extraordinary Achievement in Architecture**
Washington Metropolitan Chapter/
American Institute of Architects
Market Square, Washington, DC
1991

**Citation of Achievement**
Providence (RI) Preservation Society
John Carter Brown Library,
Providence, Rhode Island
1991

**Domino's Top 30 Architects**
1990

**National Honor Award**
American Institute of Architects
Folger Shakespeare Library,
Washington, DC
1989

**Award for Excellence for Extraordinary Achievement in Architecture**
Washington Metropolitan Chapter/
American Institute of Architects
Chrysler Museum, Norfolk, Virginia
1989

**Distinctive Residential Architecture Award**
Washington Metropolitan Chapter/
American Institute of Architects
and *Washingtonian* magazine
Residence, Washington, DC
1989

**Architectural Firm Award**
American Institute of Architects
1988

**Federal Design Achievement Award**
Presidential Design Awards
US Embassy Office Building,
Kuala Lumpur, Malaysia
1988

**Merit Award for Extraordinary
Achievement in Architecture**
Washington Metropolitan Chapter/
American Institute of Architects
HEB Grocery Company Headquarters,
San Antonio, Texas
1988

**Tucker Award**
Building Stone Institute
1001 Pennsylvania Avenue,
Washington, DC
1987

**Annual Award for Historic Preservation**
National Trust for Historic Preservation
Sumner Square/Sumner School,
Washington, DC
1987

**Excellence in Architecture Award**
Washington Metropolitan Chapter/
American Institute of Architects
St Patrick's Episcopal Church,
Washington, DC
1987

**First Award for Architecture**
Mayor of the District of Columbia
Folger Shakespeare Library,
Washington, DC
1987

**First Award for Architecture**
Mayor of the District of Columbia
Sear's House (Apex Building),
Washington, DC
1987

**Merit Award for Architecture**
Mayor of the District of Columbia
1001 Pennsylvania Avenue,
Washington, DC
1987

**Merit Award for Architecture**
Mayor of the District of Columbia
St Patrick's Episcopal Church and
Day School, Washington, DC
1987

**Citation for Architecture**
Mayor of the District of Columbia
4250 Connecticut Avenue/
Van Ness Station, Washington, DC
1987

**First Award**
Masonry Institute
St Patrick's Episcopal Church and
Day School, Washington, DC
1986

**Award of Merit**
Masonry Institute
Sumner Square/Sumner School,
Washington, DC
1986

**First Award for Historic Preservation**
Washington Metropolitan Chapter/
American Institute of Architects
Sumner Square/Sumner School,
Washington, DC
1986

**Special Award**
San Antonio (TX) Conservation Society
HEB Grocery Company Headquarters,
San Antonio, Texas
1986

**Merit Award for Architecture**
Mayor of the District of Columbia
Residence, Washington, DC
1986

**Citation for Architecture**
Mayor of the District of Columbia
Sumner Square/Sumner School,
Washington, DC
1986

**Award of Excellence**
American Institute of Architects
and American Library Association
Folger Shakespeare Library,
Washington, DC
1985

**Excellence in Architecture Award**
Washington Metropolitan Chapter/
American Institute of Architects
US Embassy Office Building,
Kuala Lumpur, Malaysia
1985

**Distinctive Residential
Architecture Award**
Washington Metropolitan Chapter/
American Institute of Architects
and *Washingtonian* magazine
Foster Residence, McLean, Virginia
1985

**Merit Award for Historic Preservation**
Washington Metropolitan Chapter/
American Institute of Architects
Dumbarton Oaks Renovation and
Addition, Washington, DC
1984

**Citation for Historic Preservation**
Washington Metropolitan Chapter/
American Institute of Architects
Apex Building Renovation and Addition,
Washington, DC
1984

**Annual Interiors Award**
*Interiors* magazine
Folger Shakespeare Library,
Washington, DC
1984

**National Honor Award**
American Institute of Architects
Immanuel Presbyterian Church,
McLean, Virginia
1983

**Non-Residential Design Award**
American Institute of Architects
and American Wood Council
Immanuel Presbyterian Church,
McLean, Virginia
1983

**Masonry Excellence Award**
Masonry Institute
4250 Connecticut Avenue/
Van Ness Station, Washington, DC
1983

**Award of Excellence**
Mid-Atlantic Region/American
Institute of Architects
Folger Shakespeare Library,
Washington, DC
1983

**Award of Excellence**
Mid-Atlantic Region/American
Institute of Architects
US Embassy Office Building,
Kuala Lumpur, Malaysia
1983

**Excellence in Architecture Award**
Washington Metropolitan Chapter/
American Institute of Architects
4250 Connecticut Avenue/
Van Ness Station, Washington, DC
1983

**Excellence in Architecture Award**
Washington Metropolitan Chapter/
American Institute of Architects
Foster Residence, McLean, Virginia
1983

**Excellence in Architecture Award**
Washington Metropolitan Chapter/
American Institute of Architects
Zapruder Residence,
Chevy Chase, Maryland
1983

**First Award for Historic Preservation**
Washington Metropolitan Chapter/
American Institute of Architects
Folger Shakespeare Library,
Washington, DC
1983

**Citation for Historic Preservation**
Washington Metropolitan Chapter/
American Institute of Architects
Sumner Square/Sumner School,
Washington, DC (Project)
1983

**First Award**
American Plywood Association
Immanuel Presbyterian Church,
McLean, Virginia
1982

**Excellence in Architecture Award**
Washington Metropolitan Chapter/
American Institute of Architects
National Humanities Center,
Raleigh, North Carolina
1982

**Distinctive Residential
Architecture Award**
Washington Metropolitan Chapter/
American Institute of Architects
and *Washingtonian* magazine
Remodeling and Addition,
Washington, DC
1982

**National Honor Award**
American Institute of Architects
National Permanent Building,
Washington, DC
1981

**Merit Award**
American Institute of Architects
and Interfaith Forum on Religion,
Art and Architecture
Immanuel Presbyterian Church,
McLean, Virginia
1981

**Excellence in Architecture Award**
Washington Metropolitan Chapter/
American Institute of Architects
Immanuel Presbyterian Church,
McLean, Virginia
1981

**Excellence in Architecture Award**
Washington Metropolitan Chapter/
American Institute of Architects
Residence, Washington, DC
1981

**Excellence in Architecture Award**
Washington Metropolitan Chapter/
American Institute of Architects
Saltonstall Stable,
Rappahannock County, Virginia
1981

**First Award for Historic Preservation**
Washington Metropolitan Chapter/
American Institute of Architects
Gallery Row, Washington, DC (Project)
1981

**Merit Award for Historic Preservation**
Washington Metropolitan Chapter/
American Institute of Architects
Apex Building Renovation and Addition,
Washington, DC (Project)
1981

**First Honor Award/**
**Homes for Better Living**
American Institute of Architects
and *housing* magazine
Residence, Washington, DC
1981

**Distinctive Residential**
**Architecture Award**
Washington Metropolitan Chapter/
American Institute of Architects
and *Washingtonian* magazine
Zapruder Residence,
Chevy Chase, Maryland
1981

**Merit Award for Historic Preservation**
Washington Metropolitan Chapter/
American Institute of Architects
1001 Pennsylvania Avenue,
Washington, DC (Project)
1980

**Merit Award for Historic Preservation**
Washington Metropolitan Chapter/
American Institute of Architects
"Kennersley", Queen Anne's County,
Maryland
1980

**Excellence in Architecture Award**
Washington Metropolitan Chapter/
American Institute of Architects
National Permanent Building,
Washington, DC
1979

**Excellence in Architecture Award**
Washington Metropolitan Chapter/
American Institute of Architects
Residence, Potomac, Maryland
1979

**Excellence in Architecture Award**
Washington Metropolitan Chapter/
American Institute of Architects
Watts Residence, Washington, DC
1979

**Excellence in Architecture Award**
Washington Metropolitan Chapter/
American Institute of Architects
Stable, Rock Creek Park,
Washington, DC
1979

**Citation for Historic Preservation**
Washington Metropolitan Chapter/
American Institute of Architects
Cox Residence, Washington, DC
1978

**Citation for Historic Preservation**
Washington Metropolitan Chapter/
American Institute of Architects
Kenney Residence, Washington, DC
1978

**Design Award**
Concrete Reinforcing Steel Institute
National Permanent Building,
Washington, DC
1977

**Merit Award for Historic Preservation**
Washington Metropolitan Chapter/
American Institute of Architects
Folger Shakespeare Library,
Washington, DC (Project)
1977

**Citation for Historic Preservation**
Washington Metropolitan Chapter/
American Institute of Architects
National Bookstore, Washington, DC
1977

**Honor Award**
Potomac Valley Chapter/
American Institute of Architects
Residence, Potomac, Maryland
1976

**First Honor Award/**
**Homes for Better Living**
American Institute of Architects
and *House & Home* magazine
Residence, Potomac, Maryland
1976

**Merit Award**
Potomac Valley Chapter/
American Institute of Architects
Pyramid Gallery, Washington, DC
1974

**International Award for Masonry Architecture**
First Biennial Louis Sullivan Award
1972

**Honor Award**
Potomac Valley Chapter/
American Institute of Architects
Euram Building, Washington, DC
1972

**Honor Award**
Potomac Valley Chapter/
American Institute of Architects
Dormitory, Mount Vernon College,
Washington, DC
1972

**Merit Award**
Potomac Valley Chapter/
American Institute of Architects
Stable, Rock Creek Park,
Washington, DC
1972

**National Honor Award**
American Institute of Architects
Chapel, Mount Vernon College,
Washington, DC
1971

**Honor Award**
American Institute of Architects
and American Association
of Junior Colleges
Chapel, Mount Vernon College,
Washington, DC
1971

**Award for Excellence in Architecture**
Board of Trade/District of Columbia
Euram Building, Washington, DC
1971

**Award for Excellence in Architecture**
Board of Trade/District of Columbia
Chapel, Mount Vernon College,
Washington, DC
1971

**National Honor Award**
American Institute of Architects
Residence, Chevy Chase, Maryland
1970

**Award of Merit**
American Institute of Architects
and American Association
of Junior Colleges
Master Plan, Mount Vernon College,
Washington, DC
1970

**Honor Award**
Potomac Valley Chapter/
American Institute of Architects
Chapel, Mount Vernon College,
Washington, DC
1970

**Honor Award**
Potomac Valley Chapter/
American Institute of Architects
Leventhal Residence, Washington, DC
1970

**Honor Award**
Potomac Valley Chapter/
American Institute of Architects
Tennis Club, St Alban's School,
Washington, DC
1970

**Award for Excellence in Architecture**
Board of Trade/District of Columbia
Fairfax Village Recreation Center,
Washington, DC
1969

**Honor Award**
Potomac Valley Chapter/
American Institute of Architects
Residence, Chevy Chase, Maryland
1968

**Award for Excellence in Architecture**
Board of Trade/District of Columbia
Tager Residence, Bethesda, Maryland
1967

## Exhibitions

**Hartman-Cox Firm Work**
American Institute of Architects,
Washington, DC
1988

**The Architecture of Hartman-Cox Architects**
Design Center,
Washington, DC
1988

**A Decade of Washington Architecture**
Athenaeum,
Alexandria, Virginia
1988

**Princeton Architectural Drawings**
Institute of Architecture and
Urban Studies,
New York, New York
1977

**Exhibition of College Architecture**
American Institute of Architects
and American Association of Community
and Junior Colleges
Washington, DC
1976

**Award Winning Architecture by Yale
Graduates**
Yale University,
New Haven, Connecticut
1976

**The Work of Hartman-Cox**
University of Virginia,
Charlottesville, Virginia
1973

# Bibliography

Abercrombie, Stanley. "Zig-zag Dorm." *Architecture Plus* (December 1973): pp. 24–29. (Mount Vernon College Dormitory)

"'Ah, to Build, to Build!': First Annual Mayor's Awards Honor the 'Noblest of All Arts'." *Washington Post* (June 9, 1986): p. WB29. (Sumner School Complex et al.)

"AIA Honor Awards 1981: Complex, Muscular Facades on Pennsylvania Avenue." *AIA Journal* (Mid-May 1981): pp. 238–239. (National Permanent Building)

"Alumni Volunteers at Georgetown Law Center: Building for the Future." *Res Ipsa Loquitur.* Georgetown University Law Center magazine (Spring/Summer 1992): pp. 5–13.

"America's Main Street." *Preservation News* (January 1981).

Annas, Teresa. "The Chrysler Comes of Age." *Virginia-Pilot/Ledger-Star* (Norfolk, February 19, 1989): p. G1.

"Architects Honor Preservation." *Preservation News* (November 1977).

*Architects of the United States of America (Volume Two).* Melbourne, Australia: Images Australia Pty Ltd, 1991, pp. 54–55.

"Architectural Firm Honored for New Design and Restoration." *Preservation Forum* (Spring 1988): p. 22. (Sumner School Complex)

"Award Winners." *Preservation News* (December 1980).

"Better Shapes for Better Living." *USIA* (April 1974).

Binney, Marcus. "Architecture: Monumental Affirmation of Faith." *Times* (London, July 17, 1990): p. 19. (Market Square, 1001 Pennsylvania Avenue, Georgetown University Law Center Library, Sumner School Complex)

Blake, Peter. "Conservative Chic." *Interior Design* (May 1988): pp. 324–325. (Architectural Firm Award)

Blake, Peter. "Opening in the Wedge." *Architectural Forum* (May 1972): pp. 32–35. (Euram Building)

Brolin, Brent C. *Architecture in Context: Fitting New Buildings with Old.* New York: Van Nostrand Reinhold, 1980, pp. 120–121 (National Permanent Building), pp. 130–131 (Dodge Center).

Bruske, Ed. "The Seven Awards for Restoration." *Washington Post* (October 29, 1978): p. G3. (Cox Residence, Kenney Residence)

"Buildings in the News: A.I.A. Names Ten Winners in Community and Junior College Awards Program." *Architectural Record* (February 1971): p. 43. (Mount Vernon College Chapel)

"Call to Arms." *Southern Accents* (July/August 1988). (HEB Headquarters Complex)

Canty, Donald J. "The Best and Worst of Washington, D.C." *Architectural Record* (February 1990): pp. 98–103. (Market Square, Georgetown University Law Center Library)

Canty, Donald and Andrea O. Dean. "Evaluation: A Small Office Building Asserts Itself, but with Respect." *AIA Journal* (September 1976): pp. 22–26. (Euram Building)

Caudill, William Wayne, et al. *Architecture and You: How to Experience and Enjoy Buildings.* New York: Whitney Library of Design/Watson-Guptill Publications, 1978, p. 41 (Mount Vernon College Dormitory), p. 94 (Mount Vernon College Chapel).

"Changing Guard at the Ol' Arsenal." *Dallas Morning News* (October 2, 1985). (HEB Headquarters Complex)

"Chapel in the Dell." *Architectural Forum* (March 1971): pp. 56–59. (Mount Vernon College Chapel)

Cheney, Margaret. "Prize-Winning Homes." *Washingtonian* (May 1985): pp. 272–276. (Foster Residence)

"Chrysler Museum Renewed." *Southern Accents* (November/December 1989).

Conroy, Sarah Booth. "Letting in the 20th Century." *Washington Post* (October 29, 1978): p. G1. (Cox Residence, Kenney Residence)

Conroy, Sarah Booth. "Praising Neighborly Buildings." *Washington Post* (October 22, 1977): p. C1. (Folger Library Addition, Visitors' Center Bookstore)

Conroy, Sarah Booth. "Present Praise, Past Panes." *Washington Post* (June 14, 1981): p. E1. (Washington Chapter AIA Awards)

Conroy, Sarah Booth. "The In(Side) and Out(Side) of Winning Architecture." *Washington Post* (March 28, 1976): p. G1. (Potomac, Maryland, Residence)

Conroy, Sarah Booth. "The Rescued & the Rescuers." *Washington Post* (November 15, 1981): p. E2. (Apex Building, Gallery Row)

Conway, Patricia L. "A New Look for District Playgrounds." *Potomac Magazine (of the Washington Post)* (June 18, 1967): pp. 22–24, 27. (Fairfax Village Recreational Center)

Cowin, Dana. "The Biggest Little Museum." *House & Garden* (June 1989): p. 41. (Chrysler Museum)

Cox, Warren J. (ed.). *Brick Architectural Details.* McLean, Virginia: Brick Institute of America, pp. 22–25. (Mount Vernon College Dormitory, Euram Building)

Cox, Warren J. "The Secretary of the Interior's Standards for Rehabilitation." *Preservation Forum* (Summer 1988).

Crosbie, Michael J. "Library Science: Planning for Book Conservation, Storage, and Information Retrieval." *Architecture* (July 1990): pp. 103–105. (John Carter Brown Addition, Folger Library Addition)

Crosbie, Michael J. "Old Made New, New Amid Old, Etc." *Architecture* (November 1983): pp. 56–57. (Folger Library Addition)

Crosbie, Michael J. "On the Avenue." *Architecture* (April 1991): pp. 58–62. (Market Square)

"Cross-Sectional Selection of Award Winners from Around the Nation." *AIA Journal* (Mid-May 1982): p. 287. (Remodeling and Addition, Washington, DC)

Dean, Andrea Oppenheimer. "An Amalgam of Styles in a Witty 'Spec' Building." *Architecture* (December 1983): pp. 68–73. (4250 Connecticut Avenue)

Dean, Andrea Oppenheimer. "Firm of the Year: Hartman Cox Very Much of Washington, D.C." *Architecture* (February 1988): pp. 44–55.

Dean, Andrea Oppenheimer. "Intricate Composition of Stepped Facades." *Architecture* (November 1986): pp. 64–65. (1001 Pennsylvania Avenue)

Dean, Andrea Oppenheimer. "Pert and Plainspoken Sanctuary." *AIA Journal* (Mid-May 1981): pp. 158–165. (Immanuel Presbyterian Church)

Dean, Andrea Oppenheimer. "Seamless Addition." *Architecture* (June 1990): pp. 74–77. (Dumbarton Oaks)

Dean, Andrea Oppenheimer. "Tall Order." *Architecture* (April 1991): pp. 64–65. (One Franklin Square)

Dean, Andrea Oppenheimer. "The Architect: Redefining Urban Renewal." *Historic Preservation* (May/June 1990): pp. 12–14. (Hartman-Cox Architects)

Dean, Andrea Oppenheimer. "Tripartite Form, Country Accent." *Architecture* (October 1983): pp. 82–85. (Foster Residence)

Dean, Andrea Oppenheimer. "Two Old Schools Woven Into an Office Complex." *Architecture* (November 1986): pp. 60–63. (Sumner School Complex)

"Design Awards/Competitions: Home for Better Living Awards." *Architectural Record* (June 1981): p. 45.

"Design for Recreation: A Traditional Campus Gets a Contemporary 'Gatehouse' in an Unlikely Place." *Architectural Record* (November 1975): pp. 130–131. (St. Alban's Tennis Club)

"Design Watch: The Art of Looking." *House Beautiful* (October 1992): pp. 70, 74–75. (Winterthur Museum Addition)

"Designing with History: Recent D.C. Architecture." *Design Action* (August 1978).

De Vido, Alfredo. *Designing Your Client's House.* New York: Whitney Library of Design/Watson-Guptill Publications, 1983, pp. 171–174. (Phillips/Brewer Residence)

Dillon, David. "The Alamo and Other Battles." *Architecture* (March 1986): pp. 62–69. (HEB Headquarters Complex)

"Dormitory at Mount Vernon College Won Top Honor Award for Hartman-Cox Architects." *Washington Post* (January 13, 1973): p. E20.

Dorris, Virginia Kent. "Concrete into Stone." *Architecture* (July 1993): pp. 112–113. (1501 M Street)

Dixon, John Morris. "Folger Library Additions and Alterations, Washington, DC: With Respect to Cret." *Progressive Architecture* (July 1983): pp. 65–73.

Emanuel, Muriel (ed.). *Contemporary Architects.* New York: St. Martin's Press, 1980, pp. 173–175, 349–350.

Faulkner, Ray and Sarah Faulkner. *Inside Today's Home.* New York: Holt Rinehart and Winston, 1975.

Fiene, Karen. "Signature of a City." *Portfolio: Contextualism* (Spring 1982): pp. 44–47. (Apex Building, Gallery Row, 4250 Connecticut Avenue, 1001 Pennsylvania Avenue, Sumner School Complex)

"Focus: A New Award for Masonry Design." *Architectural Forum* (October 1972): p. 6. (Louis Sullivan Award)

"Folger Shakespeare Library." *Architecture + Urbanism* (Japan, October 1981).

Forgey, Benjamin. "Adding to a Legend." *Washington Post* (March 8, 1987): p. F1. (Corcoran Office Building Addition)

Forgey, Benjamin. "Architects Nab Design Honors." *Washington Post* (November 5, 1993): p. G4. (800 North Capitol Street, 1200 K Street, John Carter Brown Library Addition)

Forgey, Benjamin. "A Special Kind of Office Building." *Washington Star* (October 12, 1971): p. A14. (Euram Building)

Forgey, Benjamin. "Bigger and Better?" *Washington Post* (November 11, 1981): p. E9. (Kennedy Center Expansion Study)

Forgey, Benjamin. "Classy Colossus at Franklin Square." *Washington Post* (February 16, 1991): p. C1.

Forgey, Benjamin. "Designs on the Avenue: The Four Sides of a Square." *Washington Post* (September 29, 1984): p. C1. (Market Square)

Forgey, Benjamin. "Folger Wins AIA Honor Award." *Washington Post* (May 3, 1989): p. D4.

Forgey, Benjamin. "Hartman and Cox, Getting Their Due." *Washington Post* (February 6, 1988): p. G1. (Architectural Firm Award)

Forgey, Benjamin. "It Began with Mr. Mullet's Infant Asylum." *Washington Star* (February 23, 1977): p. C7. (National Permanent Building)

Forgey, Benjamin. "Lucky Seventh: Rebirth of a Street." *Washington Post* (March 3, 1984): p. C1. (Gallery Row)

Forgey, Benjamin. "Many Rooms with Many Views." *Washington Post* (December 31, 1989): p. G4.

Forgey, Benjamin. "Market Square's Great Outdoors." *Washington Post* (August 10, 1991): p. C1.

Forgey, Benjamin. "Meeting a Massive Challenge." *Washington Post* (March 26, 1983): p. C1. (4250 Connecticut Avenue)

Forgey, Benjamin. "On Indiana, a Better Idea." *Washington Post* (August 11, 1990): p. C1. (Pennsylvania Plaza)

Forgey, Benjamin. "Our Town, Revisited." *Washington Post* (May 18, 1991): p. G1. (Market Square, Gallery Row)

Forgey, Benjamin. "Overcoming Art Cramp." *Washington Star* (September 18, 1973): p. D3. (Pyramid Gallery)

Forgey, Benjamin. "Pennsylvania Avenue." *Washington Post* (May 23, 1982): p. K1. (1001 Pennsylvania Avenue, Apex Building)

Forgey, Benjamin. "Street Wise." *Washington Post* (December 5, 1981): p. C1. (Sumner School Complex)

Forgey, Benjamin. "Sum of the Sumner." *Washington Post* (September 14, 1985): p. C1.

Forgey, Benjamin. "The Beauty on the Corner." *Washington Post* (June 13, 1992): p. C1. (1501 M Street)

Forgey, Benjamin. "The Chrysler Museum, Suddenly Splendid." *Washington Post* (February 26, 1989): p. G1.

Forgey, Benjamin. "The Gabled, Graceful Pride of St. Patrick's." *Washington Post* (July 12, 1986): p. D1.

Forgey, Benjamin. "The Law Library, One for the Books." *Washington Post* (April 15, 1989): p. C1. (Georgetown University Law Center Library)

Forgey, Benjamin. "The Pennsylvania Avenue Showdown." *Washington Post* (July 26, 1986): p. G1. (1001 Pennsylvania Avenue)

Forgey, Benjamin. "The Sky's the Limit." *Washington Post Magazine* (January 26, 1992): pp. 12–16, 26. (Franklin Square, 1501 M Street, Sumner School Complex, Euram Building, Pennsylvania Plaza)

Forgey, Benjamin. "The Well-Rounded Market Square." *Washington Post* (November 3, 1990): p. D1.

Forgey, Benjamin. "Washington's Window Pox." *Washington Post* (August 17, 1985): p. G1. (4250 Connecticut Avenue)

Forgey, Benjamin. "When New Is Good as Old." *Washington Post* (February 5, 1983): p. C1. (Folger Library Addition)

Forgey, Benjamin. "Winterthur Opens a Treasure Chest." *Washington Post* (October 10, 1982): p. D1. (Winterthur Museum Addition)

"Forty Under Forty." *Architecture + Urbanism* (Japan, January 1977): pp. 102–103. (Hartman-Cox Architects)

Freeman, Allen. "Challenge of Context in Washington." *Architecture* (November 1984): pp. 62–71. (Apex Building)

Freeman, Allen. "Complex of Solid Regional Character ." *Architecture* (May 1986): pp. 118–125. (HEB Headquarters Complex)

Geracimos, Ann. "Area Architects Noted for Folger Work." *Washington Times* (May 8, 1989): p. E5.

Goldberger, Paul. "A Blend of Architectural Grace and Eccentricity." *New York Times* (February 5, 1983): p. 5. (Folger Library Addition)

Goldberger, Paul. "A Museum Exhibits a Splendid Lack of Glitz." *New York Times* (June 4, 1989): p. H33. (Chrysler Museum)

Goldberger, Paul. "A Pat on the Back for Some Modest Buildings." *New York Times* (June 18, 1989): p. H31. (Folger Library Addition/National Honor Award)

Goldberger, Paul. "Beyond Style." *New York Times Magazine* (June 6, 1976): pp. 68–69. (Potomac, Maryland, Residence)

Goldberger, Paul. "Downtown: A Monumental Problem." *New York Times* (March 14, 1985): p. B12. (1001 Pennsylvania Avenue, Market Square)

Goldberger, Paul. "Ebb and Flow of Time and Tastes Reshape Kennedy's Grand Vision." *New York Times* (January 19, 1989): p. B12. (1001 Pennsylvania Avenue, Market Square)

Goldberger, Paul. "Finding the Proper Path in Rejuvenating Washington's Great Boulevard." *New York Times* (January 21, 1985): p. A14. (Apex Building, 1001 Pennsylvania Avenue, Market Square)

Goldberger, Paul. "In Washington, a Serious Design." *New York Times* (February 9, 1977): p. C26. (National Permanent Building)

Gordon, Barclay, F. "America Turns a Fresh Face Overseas." *Architectural Record* (December 1980): pp. 96–113. (Embassy, Kuala Lumpur)

Gordon, Barclay F. (ed.). *Interior Spaces Designed by Architects*. New York: McGraw Hill Book Company, 1974, pp. 72–73. (Mount Vernon College Chapel)

Gordon, Barclay F. and Charles K. Hoyt. "Building for Sport." *Architectural Record* (February 1977): pp. 115–129. (National Park Service Stable)

Gordon, Douglas E. and M. Stephanie Stubb. "The Mechanics of Building Rebirth: Structural Reconfiguration." *Architecture* (November 1986): pp. 100–101. (Gallery Row)

Greer, Nora Richter. "AIA Honor Awards 1983: Pert Sanctuary." *AIA Journal* (Mid-May 1983): p. 265. (Immanuel Presbyterian Church)

Greer, Nora Richter. "Placemaker." *Architectural Record* (November 1991): pp. 96–101. (Georgetown University Law Center Library)

"Hartman-Cox Architects: Preserving a Sense of Place." *Superstructure* (Summer 1990): p. 2. (1001 Pennsylvania Avenue)

"Hartman-Cox Wins First Sullivan Award, Praised for Preserving Visual Unity." *AIA Journal* (October 1972): p. 56.

"Hartman Residence." *American Home* (Mid-February 1968).

"Hartman Residence." *House Beautiful* (November 1969).

Henry, Helen. "Washington Couples Transform Three Rowhouses." *Sun Magazine* (of the *Baltimore Sun*) (August 23, 1970): pp. 16–18. (Hartman Residence)

"House in Maryland, by Hartman-Cox." *Architectural Record* (May 1977): pp. 119–122. (Potomac, Maryland, Residence)

"How to Work Your Way out of a Box." *House & Garden* (June 1974): pp. 47–63. (Cox Residence)

"Immanuel Presbyterian Church." *Architecture + Urbanism* (Japan, September 1981): pp. 29–34.

"In Architecture, Too, Anything Goes." *U.S. News & World Report* (August 1, 1983): pp. 58–59. (Immanuel Presbyterian Church/ National Honor Award)

Jenkins, Mark. "Back from the Future: From Bauhaus to Our Town with Hartman-Cox." *City Paper* (Washington, DC, July 29, 1988): pp. 14–16.

"Kaleidoscope: A Brief Review of Some Buildings Employing Elements of Daylight Design." *AIA Journal* (September 1979): pp. 76–85. (Mount Vernon College Chapel)

Kay, Jane Holtz. "Folger Library Addition: The Challenge of Adding to an Old and Venerated Building." *Christian Science Monitor* (April 15, 1983): p. 11.

"Keeping the Building in Mind." *Interior Design* (July 1978): pp. 118–121. (National Permanent Building)

"Kenney Residence." *Sunset Magazine* (Fall/Winter 1974).

"Kirche in McLean, USA." *Baumeister* (Germany, October 1982): pp. 1000–1001. (Immanuel Presbyterian Church)

Kniffel, Leonard. "Inside Storeys: AL's Annual Look at Library Facilities and Furnishings." *American Libraries* (April 1991): pp. 292–3, 295. (Georgetown University Law Center Library)

Knight, Carleton III. "Embassy Row: Designer Diplomacy." *Regardie's* (August/ September 1983): pp. 89–91. (US Embassy Office Building)

Knight, Carleton III. "National Permanent Building: Hanging Out." *Progressive Architecture* (December 1977): pp. 54–57.

Knight, Carleton III. "News Report: In Progress, Washington, DC." *Progressive Architecture* (September 1982): p. 82. (4250 Connecticut Avenue)

Knight, Carleton III. "News Report: Report from Washington." *Progressive Architecture* (September 1980): pp. 50–52. (1001 Pennsylvania Avenue)

Knight, Carleton III. "Postmodern What?" *United* (United Airlines Magazine) (June 1984): pp. 60–63. (4250 Connecticut Avenue)

Knight, Carleton III. "The US Chancery in Malaysia: Neither Fortress nor Hut." *Architecture* (July 1986): pp. 62–69.

Knight, Carleton III. "Washington, DC: An Architecture Tour." *Portfolio* (June/July 1979): pp. 92–94. (National Permanent Building)

Krantz, Les. *American Architects.* New York: Facts On File, 1989, p. 59–61.

Lacy, Bill. 100 *Contemporary Architects.* New York: Harry N. Abrams, 1991, pp. 100–101.

Laine, Christian K. "New Architecture in Washington, D.C." *Metropolitan Review* (Summer 1988): pp. 15–79. (Franklin Square, 1001 Pennsylvania Avenue, Pennsylvania Plaza, Market Square, Sumner School Complex, Corcoran Office Building Addition, Georgetown University Law Center Library, Gallery Row)

Lane, Leonard. "H.E.B. Pulls Out the Artillery for Its Supermarket Offices." *Texas Architect* (November/December 1985): pp. 104–109. (HEB Headquarters Complex)

Langdon, Philip. *American Houses.* New York: Stewart, Tabori & Chang, 1987, pp. 68–69. (Foster Residence)

Le Sueur, Dorothy. "Architects Approve Sensible Tweed Suits." *Potomac Magazine* (of the *Washington Post*) (February 15, 1970): pp. 16–17. (Leventhal Residential Addition, Hartman-Cox Offices)

"Letting the Sun Shine In." *Potomac Magazine* (of the *Washington Post*) (April 11, 1971): pp. 14–15. (Phillips/Brewer Residence)

"Leventhal Residential Addition." *Architecture + Urbanism* (Japan, November 1973).

Levin, Stephen. "Non-res Rescue: Store-to-Office Conversion Saves a Sinking Project." *housing* (June 1980): p. 34. (Dodge Center)

Lieberman, Herbert (ed.). *Award Winning Architecture/USA.* Philadelphia: ARTISTS/ USA, Inc., 1973, p. 39 (Mount Vernon College Dormitory), p. 132 (National Park Service Stable), p.184 (Euram Building).

Liebman, Rosanna. "A Genteel Lesson in Urban Sprawl." *Architecture* (February, 1988): pp. 56–61. (Monroe Hall Addition)

"Lincoln Square." *Architecture + Urbanism* (Japan, August 1982): p. 107. (1001 Pennsylvania Avenue)

Lundberg, Madeleine. "A New Bustle for Victoria." *Potomac Magazine* (of the *Washington Post*) (December 7, 1969): pp. 82–83, 85. (Scheman Residential Addition)

Lundberg, Madeleine. "Georgetown for Two." *Potomac Magazine* (of the *Washington Post*) (August 17, 1969): p. 28. (Cox Residence)

Lundberg, Madeleine. "The Forgotten American Room." *Potomac Magazine* (of the *Washington Post*) (November 23, 1969): pp. 60–61. (Tager Residence, Bathroom)

Lundberg, Madeleine. "Wicker--A 19th Century Favorite Is Back in Vogue in the Twentieth." *Potomac Magazine* (of the *Washington Post*) (June 1, 1969): pp. 36–37. (Symington Residential Addition)

"Making Room for McIntire." *University of Virginia Alumni News* (July/August 1987). (Monroe Hall Addition)

MacPherson, Myra. "Awards for Excellence in Architecture." *Washington Post* (November 18, 1971): p. C1. (Mount Vernon College Chapel)

Maroon, Fred J. *Maroon on Georgetown.* Charlottesville, Virginia: Thomasson, Grant & Howell, 1985, pp. 60–63. (Cox Residence)

Maroon, Fred J. "Inside the Houses of Georgetown." *Washingtonian* (November 1985): pp. 198–213. (Cox Residence)

Maschal, Richard. "Answering to Mr. Jefferson." *Southern Accents* (June 1991): pp. 36–38, 40–41. (Monroe Hall Addition)

Mays, Vernon. "The Chrysler Museum, Norfolk: A Remarkable Transformation." *Inform* (Virginia Society of the American Institute of Architects) (July/August 1990): pp. 18–19.

Milford, Maureen. "Fixing a Showcase's Flaws." *New York Times* (October 6, 1991): p. R5. (Winterthur Museum Addition)

Miller, Nory. "Design Directions: Looking for What is 'Missing'." *Architecture* (Mid-May 1978): pp. 153–159. (National Permanent Building)

Miller, Nory. "Monastic Retreat for Secular Scholarship." *AIA Journal* (Mid-May 1979): pp. 118–125. (National Humanities Center)

Miller, Robert L. "Pennsylvania Avenue: What Went Wrong?" *Historic Preservation* (September/October 1987): pp. 60–67. (Apex Building, 1001 Pennsylvania Avenue, Market Square, Gallery Row)

"Missed Opportunities." *Warfield's* (August 1988). (Commerce Place)

Morgan, Ann Lee and Colin Naylor (eds). *Contemporary Architects* (second edition). Chicago: St. James Press, 1987, pp. 193–195, 390.

Morris, Philip. "Enduring Appeal in New Places." *Southern Living* (September 1992): pp. 64–71. (Market Square)

Morris, Philip. "Pennsylvania Ave.: Making an American Place." *Southern Living* (September 1987): pp. 66–71. (Apex Building, 1001 Pennsylvania Avenue, Market Square)

Morton, David. "Union Station, Washington, DC: A Terminal Case." *Progressive Architecture* (November 1977): pp. 58–61. (Visitors' Center Bookstore)

Morton, David. "Waterfront Development: The Battle for Georgetown." *Progressive Architecture* (June 1975): pp. 58–61. (Dodge Center)

"Mount Vernon College: Growing Gracefully." *Progressive Architecture* (June 1972): pp. 84–87.

Mullinax, Gary. "The Galleries: Winterthur's New Way to See the Old." *News Journal* (Wilmington, Delaware, October 9, 1992): Special section, 20 pages.

"National Permanent Building Financed." *Washington Post* (March 27, 1976): p. D24.

"New Materials—and New Uses for Old Materials: Five Washington Area Architects Give Their Opinions." *Potomac Magazine* (of the *Washington Post*) (September 18, 1966): pp. 38–46.

"News Report: Bookstore a Plus for Union Station." *Progressive Architecture* (December 1976): p. 37.

"News Report: In Progress: Museums." *Progressive Architecture* (August 1983): p. 46. (Chrysler Museum)

"1989 AIA Honor Awards."
*Architecture* (May 1989): pp. 138–139.
(Folger Library Addition)

"1970 Honor Awards."
*AIA Journal* (June 1970): pp. 79–93.
(Phillips/Brewer Residence)

"1971 Community and Junior College Design
Awards." *AIA Journal* (February 1971):
pp. 26–29. (Mount Vernon College Chapel)

"Nostalgia Wins the Architects' Accolade."
*US News & World Report* (August 3, 1981):
pp. 58–59. (National Permanent Building/
National Honor Award)

Oehrlein, Mary and Baird Smith.
"Preservation Technology at Gallery Row."
*Design Action* (September/October 1982):
p. 14.

"Omnibuildings, Projects, and Visions."
*Progressive Architecture* (July 1968): p. 117.
(Mount Vernon College Master Plan)

Pearson, Clifford A. "Cheek by Jowl."
*Architectural Record* (August 1991): pp. 76–83.
(Pennsylvania Plaza)

Pearson, Clifford A. "Order out of Chaos."
*Architectural Record* (July 1989): pp. 114–119.
(Chrysler Museum)

"Phillips/Brewer Residence." *Architecture +
Urbanism* (Japan, November 1973).

"Playground on a Hill." *Architectural Forum*
(October 1969): pp. 82–85. (Fairfax Village
Recreational Center)

Plumb, Barbara. "An Entertaining Addition."
*New York Times Magazine* (December 24,
1967): pp. 26–27. (Symington Residential
Addition)

Plumb, Barbara. "Generation Gap." *New York
Times Magazine* (November 16, 1969):
pp. 134–135. (Cox Residence)

Plumb, Barbara. *Houses Architects Live In.*
New York: Viking Press, 1977, pp. 56–59.
(Cox Residence)

Plumb, Barbara. "Open-and-Shut Case."
*New York Times Magazine* (August 24, 1969):
pp. 64–65. (Hartman Residence)

Plumb, Barbara. *Young Designs in Color.*
New York: Viking Press, 1972, pp. 42–45
(Hartman Residence), pp. 98–101 (Cox
Residence).

Pool, Mary Jane and Will Mehlhorn (eds).
*House & Garden's Book of Remodeling.*
New York: Viking Press, 1978, pp. 116–119.
(Cox Residence)

"Potomac, Maryland, Residence." *L'Industria
Delle Construzioni* (August 1978).

"Potomac, Maryland, Residence." *Sunset
Magazine* (Fall/Winter 1977).

"Preservation in Washington." *Preservation
News* (September 1987).

Preston, Bruce. "A Victory for Thoughtful,
Pragmatic Design." *Washington Times*
(April 27, 1983): p. B1. (4250 Connecticut
Avenue)

"Public Parks Go Private." *Architectural Forum*
(April 1967): p. 93. (Fairfax Village
Recreational Center)

"Putting Washington in Context."
*Warfield's* (June 1988).

"Religion in America."
*USIA* (February 1974).

Richard, Paul. "Building a Hollow Building."
*Washington Post* (March 13, 1970): p. B1.
(Euram Building)

Richard, Paul. "Designing and Redesigning."
*Washington Post* (August 2, 1973): p. B1.
(Pyramid Gallery)

Richard, Paul. "The Ritual Art of Rebirth."
*Washington Post* (September 17, 1973): p. B1.
(Pyramid Gallery)

Rogers, Patricia Dale. "Winterthur's Second
Coming." *Washington Post* (June 11, 1992):
p. WH16.

Rush, Richard D. (ed.). *The Building Systems
Integration Handbook.* Washington, DC:
American Institute of Architects/John Wiley
& Sons, 1986, pp. 90–91. (National
Permanent Building)

"Scheman Residential Addition."
*American Home* (May 1969).

Scott, Pamela and Antoinette J. Lee.
*Buildings of the District of Columbia.* New York:
Oxford University Press, 1993, pp. 57–58,
146–147, 189, 197, 222–223, 227, 320–321,
375, 394, 402–403.

"Sears Sets Up Shop on America's Main
Street." *Corporate Design & Realty* (April
1985). (Apex Building)

"Setting the Stage for Plants Indoors."
*Sunset Magazine* (Fall/Winter 1974).
(Kenney Residence)

"Sleek Skins and Structural Bones."
*Fortune* (February 1973):
pp. 83–89. (Euram Building)

Sloan, Bill. *The Pursuit Of Excellence: The Story
of the Beck Companies.* Dallas, Texas: HCB
Contractors, 1987, p. 100. (Sumner Square
Complex)

Staebler, Wendy W. *Architectural Detailing in
Contract Interiors.* New York: Whitney Library
of Design/Watson-Guptill Publications, 1988,
pp. 85, 112–113, 177, 202–203
(1001 Pennsylvania Avenue), pp. 160–161
(St. Patrick's Episcopal Church).

"Stair and Rail Ideas ... If You Plan Ups and
Downs." *Sunset Magazine* (Summer, 1979).
(Washington, DC, Residence)

Stern, Robert A. M. *Modern Classicism.*
New York: Rizzoli International Publications,
1988, pp. 192–193. (Folger Library Addition)

Stubbs, M. Stephanie. "Attention to Its
Users." *Architecture* (December 1989):
pp. 54–57. (HEB Headquarters Complex)

Sullivan, Thomas D. "'Visions' of Great and
Small Futures for District." *Washington Times*
(October 4, 1992): p. D8. (Corcoran Office
Building Addition)

"Symington Residential Addition."
*American Home* (November 1967).

"Symington Residential Addition."
*House Beautiful* (May 1968).

"Symington Residential Addition."
*Sunset Magazine* (Special/Fall 1978).

"The Campus: Architecture's Showplace."
*USIA* (September 1973).

"The Exploded Square." *Sunday Magazine
(of the Washington Star)* (October 5, 1969):
p. 34–37. (Phillips/Brewer Residence)

"The 1971 Honor Awards." *AIA Journal*
(June 1971): pp. 45–55. (Mount Vernon
College Chapel)

"The Urge to Change." *House & Garden*
(June 1973): pp. 41–55. (Watts Residential
Addition)

"30 Years of Excellence in Architectural
Design: 1992 Masonry Design Awards."
*Brick & Block (*magazine of the Masonry
Institute*)* (Fall 1992). (South Parking
Structure)

"Under One Roof: Personal Space for Three
Generations." *House & Garden* (April 1969):
pp. 112–119. (Phillips/Brewer Residence)

Van Dyne, Larry. "The Mind of an Architect." *Washingtonian* (September 1984): pp. 133–141, 197–200. (Hartman-Cox Architects)

"Visitors' Center Bookstore." *Architecture + Urbanism* (Japan, October 1981).

Vollman, June R. "Three Custom House Winners." *House & Home* (September 1976): pp. 102–106. (Potomac, Maryland, Residence)

Vollman, June R. and Barbara Behrens Gers. "1981 HFBL Winners." *housing* (September 1981): pp. 57–73. (Washington, DC, Residential Addition).

Von Eckardt, Wolf. "Rating Washington's Architecture." *Potomac Magazine* (of the *Washington Post*) (January 6, 1974): pp. 18–21, 31–33. (Euram Building)

Von Eckardt, Wolf. "Something Old, Something New." *Washington Post* (May 10, 1980): p. D1. (1001 Pennsylvania Avenue)

Von Eckardt, Wolf. "Touch of Greatness." *Washington Post* (October 23, 1971): p. E1. (Mount Vernon College Chapel, Euram Building)

Walters, Jonathan. "Ventures: Battle Plan for a Texas Arsenal." *Historic Preservation* (July/August 1986): pp. 54–55. (HEB Headquarters Complex)

"Washington, D.C.: Urban Shape and Architecture." *Abitare* (July/August 1988): pp. 95–238. (Folger Library Addition, National Permanent Building, Sumner School Complex, 1001 Pennsylvania Avenue)

Washington Metropolitan Chapter/AIA. *A Guide To The Architecture of Washington, DC* (second edition). New York: McGraw-Hill Book Company, 1974, pp. 122, 139, 185, 188, 195, 199.

Whitcomb, Clorinda. "Addenda." *Potomac Magazine* (of the *Washington Post*) (March 10, 1968): p. 18. (Scheman Residential Addition)

"Who Says Washington Isn't a Major Cultural Center?" *Museum & Arts* (November/December 1988).

"Williams Library Opens." *Res Ipsa Loquitur* (Georgetown University Law Center magazine) (Winter/Spring 1989): pp. 18–23. (Georgetown University Law Center Library)

Williamson, John B. "Office Space Market Hot." *Washington Post* (April 10, 1976): p. E1. (Dodge Center)

"Winterthur Builds Elbow Room." *News Journal* (Wilmington, Delaware, September 24, 1989): p. H1.

Wright, Sylvia Hart. *Highlights Of Recent American Architecture*. Metuchen, New Jersey: The Scarecrow Press, 1982, pp. 49–50.

Wright, Sylvia Hart. *Sourcebook of Contemporary North American Architecture*. New York: Van Nostrand Reinhold, 1989, pp. 48–50. (Mount Vernon College Chapel, National Permanent Building)

"Young Architects on Their Own." *Architectural Record* (December 1972): pp. 86–103. (Tennis Stadium)

Zelenko, Lori Simmons. "Fifth Annual Interiors Awards: Shakespeare Drama." *Interiors*. (January 1984): pp. 144–145. (Folger Library Addition)

Zevon, Susan and Katie Ridder (eds). "Merging With the Garden." *House Beautiful* (September 1990): pp. 111–112, 115, 120. (Sant Residence)

# Acknowledgments

We would like to thank Richard Guy Wilson for his critical overview of our work, Andrea Dean for her major contributions to the text (and all her articles on Hartman-Cox over the years), and Marian Holmes, our office manager, who had the tedious task of compiling the bibliography and all the lists. Alessina Brooks of The Images Publishing Group produced the book by remote control, mail and fax machine with tact and efficiency.

Especial thanks must go to the photographers who have succeeded in making our buildings much better than they are in reality and who have so generously allowed their work to appear in this book.

Not least in importance in their contribution to the work illustrated in this book are two indispensable groups of people: our clients who had the confidence in our abilities to hire us and our associated architects, our consultants and our own staff who executed so much of the work. We thank you both.

## Photography Credits

# Index

Bold page numbers refer
to projects included in
Selected and Current Works.